DADDY'S MILK

By
Emerson Morris

xulon PRESS

THANKS

First, I want to thank God, who is the ultimate Father, who provides the *best* milk. If it wasn't for his favor and grace I wouldn't have this platform to share my story with the world. I want to thank my beautiful wife April Morris for believing in me, without you this book wouldn't be complete. I also want to thank my gorgeous daughter, Emoni Morris for her patience in allowing me to write this book. Always remember this book is my love for you! To my father, I graciously thank you for your continual love and support you've shown to all your kids. I know millions of fathers will be healed from your story. To my mom, who passed during the completion of this book. I want to thank you for setting the foundation and breaking the cycles. You were my mother, counselor, friend, encourager, pen pal, motivator, comedian, coach, and prophet. You said it back in the fall of 1997, "God is going to give you a book for men." Well mom, this is that which has been spoken of. I love you and I promise, your legacy with never be forgotten! Finally, I want to thank every man that poured into me from my childhood, teenage years, and adult life. Please remember this book couldn't be accomplished, if it wasn't for you imparting in my life. Always remember fathers your MILK does matter!

TABLE OF CONTENTS

CHAPTER 1
DELIVERY DAY

~⌐

I t was a late Monday evening on September 1, 2008—Labor Day—at St. Joseph's Women's
Hospital in Tampa, Florida when my daughter was born. The beginning of our pregnancy
was exciting and cute, but in the last trimester, all the cuteness went out the window! Throughout
the day my wife found herself fighting her hormones, lowering the house A/C, and sending me
to the store for peanut M & M's. I can hear her saying, "Emerson, I want the bag of M & M's
with the nuts in them." Fathers, we have to realize when a pregnant woman asks for a specific
kind of food, we better meet the need or she will turn into beauty and the beast! Even though
I was aggravated from her sending me to the store at 11:00 at night and 1:00 in the morning, I
could not complain because I understood we were feeding two people.

The day before her delivery, I can remember my wife in church sitting in a rocking chair
with the expression on her face saying, "How much longer?" As we left church and arrived
home, my wife, being the patient person that she is, went in our garage and started to walk on
an inclined treadmill, while listening to a song by Dr. Juanita Bynum called, "I Don't Mind
Waiting." I was very confused. If she did not mind waiting, then why was she on an inclined
treadmill walking 3.4 speed, while 9 months pregnant? *Listen carefully! Walking on a treadmill
going 3.4 speed isn't safe for a woman that's 9 months pregnant.* I stated to her, "April do
you realize you're pregnant not with just your child, but our child?" She stated, "Medical
studies show exercising makes the delivery faster." "Yes, proper exercising!" I replied. As she
continued to exercise and began to ignore me and my facial expression, I gave in and began to

support her by exercising also. After my wife increased the treadmill incline to its highest peak, thinking the speed of the treadmill would make the delivery faster and nothing happened, we decided to prepare ourselves for bedtime. We were anxiously praying that this would be the night that our beautiful daughter, Emoni Abigail Morris would be born.

Ready With Expectation

Later that night, I had a dream that my wife's water broke all over our comfortable, intimate, and sacred bed. However, when I woke up and realized it was only a dream and my wife was on her side of the bed asleep, as if she was a newborn wrapped in a comforter, I was disappointed. *Our daughter's due date was September 7, 2008...by this time my wife was 10 months pregnant*! At 10 months pregnant I was happy that my wife was resting comfortably, but disappointed that her water didn't break. My blood pressure went from high to normal. Believe me, that morning I wanted to see some type of water on that bed. I didn't care if it was Aquafina, Zephyrhills, Smart Water or Spring Water.

After getting my emotions together from my false dream, I began to occupy my time by going downstairs to clean up the garage. Women, let me give you a first-time, anxious, expectant father's secret: if you find your husband or significant other doing chores he doesn't normally do, maybe he's anxious just like you. Example: he's washing the dishes when he normally doesn't wash them, walking the dog, cleaning out the bathroom, or watching Lifetime movies with you. Either a change has come, like Sam Cooke's 1964 single, or he has gotten a revelation like Moses on the backside of the desert. Now if he's already a father and this is his second or third child, then he's probably watching ESPN stating, "Woman how long its going take for you to deliver this baby, our first peanut didn't take this long." Women, always remember EVERY man is different. Some men like ties, others like bow ties. Some men like sushi, and others like fried chicken. So every father has different emotional thoughts during their wife or significant other's pregnancy process.

Before we knew if the child was going to be a boy or girl, I told my wife all these revelations and dreams of us having a daughter. In the dream our daughter had a fair skin tone and a head full of hair. I saw the labor room as I heard the doctor say, "It's a girl!" *Women please understand, your husband or significant other may respond in silence by exercising, washing cars, reading, or watching sports. However, realize if he's present in the home, attending as the doctor checks with you, or listening, that's a sign that he's just as excited as you.* While being internally excited, I began to clean the garage. Forty minutes went by, and my wife walked in with a calm expression on her face, stating what every responsible, mature, caring, expectant father wants to hear from his wife or baby's mother: "I'm having strong contractions or my ¹water broke."

You have to understand, my wife didn't walk in the garage door with excitement as if she was standing behind that black bus on Extreme Home Makeover. She was calm like dew in the morning in Thomasville, Georgia on an early fall day. To tell you the truth, I didn't believe her because she was so calm. After she stated the exciting news, she proceeded in the kitchen to wash dishes as if Dawn dish detergent was more important. I replied, "Woman, are you crazy? Let's go to St. Joseph's hospital and have this baby!" Before proceeding to the hospital we got all the items we needed. Packing for the delivery was like moving to a new home: do you have toothpaste, Listerine, suitcase, baby bag, wigs, wipes, and the dress for after the delivery? As I saw all these items we were bringing, I asked her, "Do you think we should take the mattress with us?" She replied, "Just relax and breathe; we're coming back home." My wife proceeded to the bathroom, combing her hair and putting makeup on her face. Now ladies, either I saw the wrong baby videos, or she's just superwoman. I replied, "April, did your water break for real?" I didn't want to make a blank trip. While she began to look at me with uncertainty, she

---

¹ Water break- it means the placenta has broken, enabling the baby to begin traveling down the birth canal–some liquid is usually released when this happens, hence the term.

hesitantly showed me evidence of her water breaking. To make sure this wasn't a false alarm, I began to play "Inspector Gadget," because I wanted this to be the day Emoni was born. After seeing what I saw, I stated, "Can you please pass the jelly? I'm just joking!" I said, "Let's go!" Driving to the hospital, my wife was sitting in the passenger seat, putting lipstick on while observing herself in the mirror. My reply to her, "Are you going to have a baby or are you auditioning for America's Next Top Model?" She said, "You never know who you may see at the hospital," and I replied, "Yeah, like a doctor."

We Will Find A Room

As we arrived at the hospital lobby, I just knew since my wife was about to have a baby we'd find a room quickly. When we arrived at the hospital I realized instantly that movies are different than real life. In the movies, the father takes his wife to the hospital, 1 to 3 nurses and doctors are there by his side coaching him through the process. However, in reality, the receptionist makes you sign your name, take your name sticker, and says, "Please have a seat, we'll be right with you." What????!!!! *There is a rapper by the name of Lil John and he has this phrase in his rap song that states, "What, Okay!!!!"* As a first time father, who has been waiting for this moment, driving to the store for 11 months picking up M&M's, the wife burning electricity on our inclined treadmill, and this receptionist tells me, "Please have a seat we will be right with you?" I stated to myself, "Where does she think we are: at Red Lobster, The Cracker Barrel, The Cheesecake Factory?" Does she know that my wife could literally deliver our daughter at any time? I almost blew a gasket! I was upset. No, I'm going to be honest; I was going to lose control like the song in Janet Jackson's album "Rhythm Nation". Fathers, she didn't understand! The baby deliveries I saw on T.V. were couples with nurses and doctor's coaching parents through their process from the time they arrived to the hospital until the baby was born. However, after having my encounter with the receptionist, I began to realize she was the only ticket to get in our assigned hospital room. I must sit down and shut my mouth.

After twenty minutes went by, we finally arrived at a room and I was praying to God that this wasn't a false alarm. While in the room, anticipating the unexpected, the doctor walked in with a glove tightly gripped to the top of her fingertips stating to my wife, "Open your legs and breathe." The nurse ran her plastic glove in between my wife's legs. I was thinking, "WOW." We don't get an introduction? Hello? What is your name? Can I buy you lunch? Who are you? What's your mother's or father's name? Just open your legs and breathe. *Huh! That's amazing; I stated the same thing the night my wife got pregnant.* Waiting for the doctor's arm to come out was like waiting for a politician to tell the truth.

Finally, the doctor pulled her glove out and stated, "We're going to deliver a baby." When I heard those words, outwardly I seemed calm, but inwardly I felt like I was in the locker room at the Super Bowl and the head coach said, "You will be starting the first quarter." I was shocked, excited, and amazed that this was going to be the day I got to see my daughter! After hearing those words I began to call my parents, in-laws, and friends. *Fathers, I was so excited I called Ghost Busters!* While getting prepared to deliver Emoni, the nurses began to bring my wife a gown; being a first time parent I thought this was the room we were going to deliver her in. However, the nurse stated, "No, the delivery room is on the second floor; dad, just sit back and relax, it's going to be a *long* day." Little did I know, but she was right! This was the start of many other long days and nights.

CHAPTER 2
THE LABOR ROOM

The Labor Room- a hospital room where a woman in labor stays before being taken to the delivery room.

Labor-activity, **chore**, daily grind, diligence, drudgery, effort, employment, endeavor, energy, exercise, exertion, grind, grunt work, industry, job, moonlight, operation, **pains,** pull, push, strain, stress, struggle, sweat, toil, **travail**

After we realized this would be the day of our daughter's birth, I was extremely excited. While we transitioned to our assigned labor room, the majority of the female nurses were patting me on my back, stating, "You're doing a great job; are there anymore men out there like you?"The expressions on their faces seemed amazed that a young father was present supporting his wife. I received so much love that I started to feel like the CEO of St. Joseph's Hospital. I was thinking to myself, this is what I'm supposed to do. This is my wife and child. I am supposed to be here, this is my assignment. I am supposed to listen when she says, "Massage my back, it's tight." She didn't get pregnant by herself. Like Bernie Mac stated in the1999 movie *Life*, "I'm that baby's pappy's."

As we arrived to our delivery room, our assigned nurse asked my wife specific health questions and proceeded to perform tests on her body. While the nurse was asking her questions like, "What's the last meal you've eaten? How do you feel? Do you have high blood pressure? Do you have any health issues?" I started to realize that delivering a baby is a matter of life and death.

The World Health Organization states:

Every minute, at least one woman dies from complications related to pregnancy or child-birth—that means 529,000 women a year. In addition, for every woman who dies in childbirth, around 20 more suffer injury, infection or disease—approximately 10 million women each year. Five direct complications account for more than 70% of maternal deaths: hemorrhage (25%), infection (15%), unsafe abortion (13%), eclampsia (very high blood pressure leading to seizures – 12%), and obstructed labor (8%).

Fathers, it is very important that we are present in the labor room for our wife, girlfriend, and significant other. Yes! Delivering a child is one of the most exciting moments for any parent, but we as "fathers" have to understand the seriousness of a mother delivering a child into this world. Men! I never truly understood the dynamics of a woman's body until I experienced the emotional process of my wife's pregnancy, which included mood swings, tiredness, morning sickness, stretch marks, and most of all, nurses having her sign documents just in case a life is lost during the birthing. In the labor room I was wondering to myself, "how in the world do some women conceive three to eight babies?" Let alone, just having one is work. The other half of me was saying, "All the emotional changes pregnant women go through, I can't see how a *man* is not there for the mother and *his* child."

Now women let me throw out this disclaimer: if you've been sleeping with multiple men and you don't know the father, then that's a burden you have to bear. However, it is unfortunate that your child has to bear that burden also. Now, I didn't say your child *is* a burden or confused. What am I saying? Making "UNSOUND" decisions and willingly conceiving from multiple men isn't fair to your child. Ladies, "YES" you can raise your child by yourself and millions of our beautiful mothers are accepting that role presently in our society. However, you didn't conceive him or her by yourself. I want to be very clear. I'm not referring to single mothers whose husbands or significant others left and didn't want to take responsibility as father, caretaker, and man. I'm referring to those mothers that don't care who their next baby father is, as long as he has money, is attractive, drives a nice car, is a rapper, athlete or seasonal drug king pen on the block. Ladies, I realize those *are strong statements but I would rather change your perception than just inspire you with no change of perception.*

Now to "US" fathers, if we put it in and you've gotten your hands, metaphorically speaking, caught in the cookie jar, then it's our responsibility to stay in the kitchen until those cookies are baked. My favorite cake is carrot cake and Publix is the only place I purchase carrot cake from; I know that before I bite into the cake, I expect the ingredients of Publix carrot cake to be fresh, soft, and rich. Men! The same way we love our special ingredients of our cake, cookies, or whatever your favorite dish is, our sons and daughters are asking us not to leave the labor room until life comes forth. Men, I don't know about you, but I hate burnt or not done cake, cookies, muffins, and especially cornbread. Let's be real, if you've ever eaten any type of food that wasn't baked properly, you may have a bad perception on the cook's cooking and the way he or she prepares their food. Men, we don't want any dessert half done, so let's not give our kids half done fathering. What do I mean by half done? Let's not give them half done time, support, helping them with their homework, communication, and love! Basically, fathers, this means we have to be in that labor room supporting our wife or significant other until she delivers not just their baby, but also our baby.

What's Your Excuse

To the father who says, "She's not my wife. This female was just a woman to have sex with on the side." Men, men, men! I don't care if getting your baby's mama pregnant was a mistake, Red Roof Inn special or backseat of a Chevy. FATHERS! If we put our Mr. Johnson in, we must take **full ownership as a father**! Now to the men that are married, since she's your wife, she shouldn't have to ask you to be in the delivery room. It should be a blessing, privilege, honor, joy, and covenant to have a family.

Genesis 2:21 states, "And the LORD God caused a deep sleep to fall upon Adam, and he slept: and he took one of his ribs, and closed up the flesh instead thereof; 22 And the rib, which the LORD God had taken from man, made he a woman, and brought her unto the man.23 And Adam said, This is now bone of my bones, and flesh of my flesh: she shall be called Woman, because she was taken out of Man.24 Therefore shall a man leave his father and his mother, and shall **cleave** unto his wife: and they shall be one flesh.25 And they were both naked, the man and his wife, and were not ashamed.

Cleave-to adhere closely; stick; cling; to remain faithful.

Husbands, our wives and children are calling us to cleave to our assignments and positions in our communities as well as family. There may be a good percentage of men that say, "I made some unsound decisions in my life as a father, and I wasn't in the labor room on my child's delivery day. I'm not worthy to read this book as a man, let alone forgive myself." FATHERS! Listen with your heart and not your head! I repeat; fathers listen with your heart, not your head!" Why do I say, don't listen with your head? In our self-thinking, our heads tell us we're not worthy to be in our child's life. That negative thought says, "Who are you to be Mr. Comeback in your child's life, you weren't there before."

http://www.fathersincorporated.com

ACTS ON ABSENT FATHERS

1. 24 million children in America—one out of three—live in homes without biological fathers.

2. A child with a nonresident father is 54 percent more likely to be poorer than his or her father.

3. Fatherless children are twice as likely to drop out of school.

4. Kindergarteners who live with single parents are over-represented among those lagging socially, emotionally and cognitively and also tend to have more health issues. Thirty-three percent of children who were behind in all three areas were living with single parents, while only 22% were not lagging behind.

5. A study of 13,986 imprisoned women showed that more than half of them grew up without their father. Forty-two percent grew up in a single-mother household, and 16 percent lived with neither parent.

6. Children growing up without fathers are at a far greater risk of child abuse:

   - A 77 percent greater risk of being physically abused

   - An 87 percent greater risk of being harmed by physical neglect

   - A 165 percent greater risk of experiencing notable physical neglect

   - A 74 percent greater risk of suffering from emotional neglect

   - An 80% greater risk of suffering serious injury as a result of abuse

   - And overall, they are at a 120 percent greater risk of being endangered by some type of child abuse

You Are Still the Father

Fathers lets just get ALL of the low self-esteem issues out of the way. You maybe a deadbeat dad, failure as a parent, selfish, self-centered, adulterer, stupid, angry, jealous, or not emotionally stable but guess what? Let's see if you're smarter than a fifth grader. Does your faults exclude you from being that child's father? No. You are still the father of that child. Men, we can't allow our emotions to take away our fatherly responsibilities. Fathers, even though you weren't present during your child's delivery day, it's never too late to reconcile the date. What do I mean by the date? Throughout our child's maturing stages from infancy to adulthood, there are going to be many delivery

dates in their lives. Dates like: birthdays, changing pampers, teaching our kids how to walk, potty training, VPK graduation, graduation from elementary school, middle school, high school, and college. Fathers, our children need us on these dates! Fathers we "ALL" have made unsound and unstable decisions, but if we can forgive ourselves and realize that our child needs us more outside of the womb than inside, we can take our eyes off of "back then" and pick up now by being consistent in our children's present and future dates. Fathers, our daughter's need our approval when that particular young man wants to marry her; our son's need counseling when he feels like there are no job opportunities in our society. Fathers, our children need us on these dates so we can make the proper sound delivery in their destiny.

The Labor Room Scene (continued)

After my wife had finished being questioned by the nurse, she replied to me, "My contractions are becoming stronger!" While breathing and pushing, our child's godparents were helping and observing with expectation. Twenty minutes throughout the laboring process, the third godparent burst through the door screaming with excitement on her face, "I brought grapes!" We all shouted with a loud, "SHHHH!" I stated to her, "We're not having a nutrition orientation, we're about to deliver a baby." As we sat in the labor room, I began to laugh while my wife started to transform from America's Next Top Model to one of those women fighting on the Jerry Springer show. Nine hours went by and Emoni was still in her mother's womb. I was sitting there wondering, "Man, delivering a baby is like waiting for a space shuttle to arrive back to Earth." Sitting in the labor room, I began to think about what my mother felt like when delivering me. During my childhood she stated to me that my father wasn't present in the labor room when I was born, but her sister by the name of Aunt B. B. was present by her side. Men, we don't think about the trials and teenage rebellion we took our mothers through until we see first what women go through during labor.

As the contractions became stronger, the temperature in the room became hot, and guys, I don't mean hot in a sexy way! There was nothing sexy up in that room, *like the teenagers say, "Ya feel me."* Men! Legs were in the air, screaming and shouting everywhere, the room temperature went from North Pole cold to Miami Heat hot. At first my wife said she's a solider, she doesn't need an epidural, but after hurricane Katrina kicked her twice she wanted that epidural immediately! The nurse made my wife turn side to side so the epidural would kick in but the contractions became stronger. I can hear it ringing in my head again and again. "Push, push, push," the nurse replied. "Dad, grab her hand and encourage her to push!" The nurse we had was "OLD SCHOOL." She didn't believe in being light handed; she was aggressive and straight to the point.

I don't know if you have ever seen the 1989, Pee Wee Herman's Big Adventure movie, but there was a female truck driver named large Marge; our nurse reminded me of Large Marge. I went to the restroom a couple of times and she stated to me, "Where do you think you're going, are you leaving her?" I said, "Look lady, I don't know what your husband, ex-husband, baby's father, boyfriend did to you, but I'm going to the restroom." While I was walking around the hallway she continued to stare at me as if I was making up a lie. When I arrived from the restroom, my wife's contractions became stronger; now my wife and the nurse were looking like those fighting women on the "Jerry Springer Show." I began to lift my wife's left leg and the nurse held the right, and the doctor was in the middle of everything. YES! I do mean everything. Three people were telling my wife to push. The hospital went from a labor room to the locker room. The only difference was that in the labor room there were all women. People were shouting, screaming, sweating, and everything else. As I was holding her left leg, I started to see multiple strings of hair from the top of the baby's head, coming from the vagina. I was anxiously waiting to see my little girl, thinking will she look like me? Will she have my skin tone, eyes, lips or smile? The other part of me was thinking, I pray it's a girl like the doctor's said because I already painted those walls pink. *Ladies let me just share what majority of expectant fathers fear: painting the baby's room all pink and the baby comes out being a boy.*

Here She Comes

My wife continued to push as if she was running a 15k, veins intensely showing from her neck. For a moment, I felt bad for her because I played a crucial role in her going through this transformation. Twenty minutes within the birthing, there it was. I say "it" because I wanted to look at the vagina to make sure she's a girl because I had already painted those walls pink. Remember? It was truly amazing to see something in seed form on a sonogram develop and be born an infant that only the hand of God could create. As chunks of blood came out of the womb and the baby was drenched with excess from the womb, I was in an emotional standstill position thinking, "My wife's vagina will never be the same!" I'm like, what else is up in there, Waldo? *Men, then there's the statement every doctor loves to say to every first time father, "Here are the scissors, and cut the cord." I was thinking to myself, "You get paid for this, you need to cut the cord."* I may cut it too long or short. Finally, as I found the courage to cut the umbilicalcord, while my wife was looking with release on her face as if she just got finished using the restroom. A look of peace had come over her because she knew the birthing was a success. Immediately after delivery, the doctor tightly swaddled Emoni with comfortable fabric, then stated to me, "Dad, it's time to hold your baby girl." I was thinking, isn't she supposed to go through an infant laboratory or something? She just arrived here on planet Earth. When I found the courage to hold my daughter for the first time it was a remarkable feeling. There were no adjectives, nouns, exclamations, no correct grammar that could describe how I felt when holding my first child. After holding beautiful Emoni Morris I then passed her to my wife. As she began to hold her, I could see the joy on her face. During this time I realized her Godparents were probably tired of me repeating, "It's amazing, amazing, amazing", as if I had energizer batteries and someone pushed play. I was so amazed from a seed into an egg, this child was born. I know that sounds elementary, but that's what is amazing about God's creation and purpose.

Chapter 3
"When Reality Sinks In"

My wife and I were so excited to deliver a baby girl weighing 7 pounds 8 ounces and 22 inches. However, as the husband, father, and man of my home, I was extremely afraid. I can hear people say, "Why were you afraid? This is your first child. You just delivered a healthy, beautiful girl!" When we were expecting our first child, I was making $38,000 in salary. Yet, I came up a couple of points short on my Teacher's Certification Exam during the process of our pregnancy, which put me in a non-instructional position as an assistant teacher. To bring you closer to my reality, after the delivery I was making $11.63 an hour as an assistant teacher with no medical insurance. To add salt to an open wound, a month earlier than Emoni was born, my wife was nine months pregnant and her department was terminated because of budget cuts. WOW! Talking about keeping the baby relaxed in the womb. When she called with the latest breaking news, outwardly I was very calm. To tell you the truth, I said, "God if you don't make a way, then I guess it's time for us to go to heaven, but if we're still living on this earth, then you're going to make a way." I wasn't trying to be religious, prophetic or Atlantic Ocean-deep; at that moment as a man, I didn't have the answers or solutions to this problem. Men! Have you ever had a problem you really don't have the solution to? No, for real! Have you ever had a problem you didn't have the solutions to? I don't know if you're a CEO, pastor, investor, marketing guy, entrepreneur, manager, Vice President, NFL player, NBA player, tennis, golfer, boxer, car racer, grandfather, father, uncle, or sibling. We as men have to realize we can't solve everything. It is challenging for many of us to look at the reality in our lives or families and say, "I don't have the solution to the problem", and especially as men.

In my early fatherhood, I was in a place mentally stating to myself, "We can't get any lower than this." When my wife walked through the door after being terminated, she was very disappointed and saddened. While she walked up the stairs into her closet, not looking to speak or be held, I just began to say to myself, "Emerson, someone has to be strong." When I mention the word STRONG, I'm not referring to benching 450 pounds strong, I'm referring to valiant STRONG, peace STRONG, taking care of your kids STRONG, loving your wife STRONG, picking up your child from daycare STRONG! While we were at home asking God for understanding and clarity because time was ticking for the birthing of Emoni, my wife got a call from her former job, stating a financial aid department wanted to offer her a position. While she contemplated on the decision to accept the offer, she called me and asked, "Do you think I should accept the position, because it pays less?" I stated to her, "Are you kidding me? Does the position have medical insurance?!!!" As soon as she stated, "yes", I said, "Call, email, text, fax, tweet, Instagram those people back immediately!"

It was amazing! A week ago, her department was let go from budget cuts and now she was going back to the same institution, but a different assignment for less pay. "When reality sinks in." From the positive side, we had insurance to deliver our daughter. Two months later Emoni finally arrived. The day after the delivery, she was screaming from the top of her lungs as if she was singing "All My Single Ladies" in the background for Beyonce. I was overwhelmed with sleep deprivation and feeling like I went through a full football practice, thinking about mortgage, HOA fees, car insurance, electricity, cable, internet, phone, student loans and wondering, how will we have enough to pay for a babysitter? Oh! Did I mention mortgage? Wow! I thought tour days in my collegiate years were tough, but fatherhood responsibility is tougher.

Will It Get Better?

So, here we are in St. Joseph's hospital room at 3:00 a.m. in the morning with the cares of life on my mind. I emotionally began to break like former heavyweight Mike Tyson unexpectedly losing to Buster Douglas. My wife was unexpectedly surprised to see me cry because she had never seen me cry. As you will read in Chapter 5, I'm not saying men aren't supposed to cry, but before that moment, she'd never seen me emotional in that way. Men, I played football in little league, high school, and on the collegiate level. The high school I attended is located in the inner city in Miami, Florida; during that time majority of the boys wore gold teeth, long dreads or sold drugs. In college, I played with 105 guys from different personalities and ethnicities. During my collegiate football career at the University of South Florida, I broke my right tribal and fibula at Raymond James Stadium. My max bench was 430 pounds and rep 225 for 29 times. I stated "ALL" that to say, "When I was sitting in that hospital room with no health insurance and my daughter forcefully screaming from the top of her lungs," I HAD NEVER BEEN SO AFRAID IN MY LIFE! You see, its one thing to go through something by yourself and it's another to go through with a family, group, or institution. Men, I don't know about you, but leading a wife or significant other is one thing. However, leading our children is another. Why? In a marriage we're dealing with grown folks, but raising a child means that child has to be nurtured, cared for, cultivated, trained, and most of all loved!

I can remember sitting in the hospital room overwhelmed with tears and God spoke to me and said, "I'm positioning you to be the voice for men that are tired, scared, suicidal, broken, and emotionally paralyzed from the cares of life." There are numerous pieces of literature and praises for the fathers who make six figures or the fathers who provide material things for their kids. What about the fathers who don't have the resources to provide the intangible things in life? However, he pours his DNA, time and spirit into his child. The father who's a positive stay-at-home dad who washes dishes, folds clothes, or even cooks. Clothes and shoes go out of style, but stamping our identity into our child is breaking negative cycles in your generation. To my fathers who don't live with their child, you shouldn't put time into your child's life just to keep your baby's mother quiet or from putting you on child support. We should love and show affection towards our children because we don't want to continue the cycle of just meeting our financial obligation, instead of building a healthy and transparent relationship with our child.

Planning to Fail

Here I am on the second day of my daughter's life; I felt like a failure. Failed! Because I felt I didn't position my family financially to be in better circumstances; failed, to pass my teacher's certification. To be very transparent men, I did fail. Listen! Not because of the position I was in materially or financially, but I failed by not preparing to be in this position. I want all men not to miss what I just said. I failed by not preparing as a husband, father, and man NOT to be in this position. Let me speak to us men.

Preparation- a proceeding, measure, or provision by which one prepares for something: preparations for a journey. 2. any proceeding, experience, or the like considered as a mode of preparing for the future.

Fathers, when we don't prepare, try, study, apply, listen, or become teachable, we don't plan. When there is no proper planning, then we as fathers consistently put our families and children in unsound positions. The truth of the matter is that I didn't plan for my teacher's certification because fathers, I feared taking the test. Ever since I was in elementary school, I struggled with reading. In the third grade I was in the Chapter 1 program. When they called on me to read I was sweating so heavy you would have thought I just got finished running a Gasparilla 15k. Going through middle school, high school, and college my reading had improved, but I just read literature just to get by. You know literature like the sports page and then the sports page again. However, years later as a grown man, I still had a fear of taking tests.

Question to all MEN? What is your fear? Is it reading, losing weight, changing eating habits, getting a check up, applying for that job or different position, applying for a loan, getting on the treadmill, budgeting, taking that class, asking your wife for forgiveness, signing up for AA treatment or a treatment center, going back to school, communicating with your wife and family, trusting other ethnicities that you're not accustomed to, counseling, getting married or trusting women or men? As a child, I always thought reading was my fear; however, getting older and understanding my emotions better, I'm realizing people don't fear doing, they're afraid to fail. Men, we must realize in order to overcome our fears we must face them and most of all try. Fathers, fear always kills preparation! Never forget fear always kills preparation! Where there is fear, there will always be procrastination. It took me 10 years to pass a specific test for my teacher's certification. I didn't take the test consistently within 10 years, I was content and comfortable on my three year temporary certification, while knowing I'll received another three year temporary certificate once I sat out as an instructional teacher for a whole year. Passing this test shouldn't have taken me ten years, but I let fear and procrastination get in the way. Many times my wife would say, "Emerson, you need to take your test, you need to take your test. Emerson, did you register for your test?" Anytime she asked me that question, I would internally get upset. Why? Because her asking me those questions made me identify my fear. Men, when I got sick and tired of being in this position, as a substitute and assistant teacher, I was bold enough to face my fears. I had to realize in order to pass this test I couldn't just try to understand the full exam, but identify the test-taking strategies, conceptual and organizational skills, word choice, sentence structure, knowledge of sense, concepts, operations, algebraic thinking, and geometry spatial sense. As I began to study, study some more, and invest my time and energy into the test-taking strategies and not just the test, I found myself passing the test, conquering, and overcoming my fears. What took me 10 years to complete from procrastination and fear, when studying the strategy with a little sacrifice of my time, took me one year to successfully complete with a passing score. Men, many of us are in horrible financial circumstances, unhealthy communication circumstances with our families, bitter circumstances with people because we fail day by day and sometimes minute by minute to face our fears. Men, when facing your fears you're looking at the test; look at the strategy. You see men, we don't have money issues, alcohol issues, over-eating issues, record issues, and charge issues. We have a vision issue.

"We" have to understand that each and every one of us has vision within us. Vision isn't external; it's internal.

Proverbs 29:18: "Where *there is* no vision, the people perish."

Let's Build With a Plan

When a company gets ready to build a building, they make plans for that development. Many times we put attention on the builders, which are very important. However, we don't appreciate the architect. Without the architect you would never SEE the vision, plan, and blueprint of the designs. Fathers, God has put vision in all of us! I don't care if you made bad decisions, are recovering from addiction, physical sickness, been divorced numerous times, or if people called you a deadbeat dad. You have to know you have vision in you. **However, until we find the vision, which is our purpose "within" us, we'll always walk in fear**. When we first find our vision, get our plan, and don't embrace fear, all things are possible. Men! We first must take ownership and say "I failed", but realize I will succeed because vision and purpose is inside of me—not just as a father, but a generational charger for my family.

Day Later After the Birthing

Later, that morning I emotionally, mentally, and spiritually got myself together. I realized I couldn't miss a day of work because I had no insurance. While driving to work the day after my daughter was born, I had mixed emotional feelings. One part of me was amazed at how God can manifest creation from sperm and egg; the other part was thinking how I allowed my family to be in this financial position. There is an old saying, "If you want to know a man's heart, check his wallet." Let me tell you, if you would have checked my wallet, you would have seen zero dollars. I was emotionally broke! Finally, as I arrived to work I was thinking about my daughter and wife. Wondering how they were doing. Wondering how my wife was adjusting emotionally. Wondering, "is she overwhelmed?" Also, I was thinking about my newborn daughter, Emoni Abigail Morris! Being at work a day after my first child was born, I decided to call my wife and newborn during work hours to see how they were doing. My wife, who could barely speak from the exhausting night, was excited to hear from me, but I could discern in her voice she wanted to rest. When the final school bell rung, I went home to take a bath, rushing to the hospital because I didn't want to feel like a deadbeat dad or like I wasn't there for my child. Arriving back to the hospital, rushing cooly through the hospital halls was like Cinderella, rushing to find her lost slippers. As I walked through the room, my wife and daughter were present in the hospital's rocking chair. I began to reach for Emoni as if she was a football, fumbling in a Miami Northwestern vs. Miami Jackson soul bowl. As I held her into my arms I was truly thankful to God for having a healthy, beautiful daughter.

CHAPTER 4
LET THE PARENTING BEGIN

During the process of my wife's pregnancy I stated to myself, "I can't wait for the delivery of our baby; it will be all over then." Huh! Little did I know this was just the beginning! You see, this was my first child; I've never babysat, let alone ever kept a newborn. As a father, parenting was all new to me. Men, parenting was so new, I felt like a prostitute wearing an all-black, tight dress walking towards the altar on first Sunday morning in a Baptist church. For those who don't understand that analogy, that's the same way I was trying to learn fatherhood. *Many of us as fathers are so excited about being the daddy, pappy, babies' daddy, or father. However, we as men have to realize that just having a daddy title doesn't make us a man! Many fathers love to express their manhood by the number of children they have sown, but we as men need to realize, understand, and embrace the importance of the commitment it takes to be a father.*

After the birthing of our daughter, my wife was in the hospital for three whole days and she was eagerly ready to go HOME! Home to sleep in our own bed, eat our own food, look at our own cable, lay on our own couch, wear our own clothes; just to be honest with you, we just wanted to leave far away from the hospital environment—three days and a half is enough for me! The hospital halls became so familiar, each walkway started to feel like the glasshouse at the fair; every father that has had their hospital experience; you know it's time to leave when you can remember the hospital daily menu for breakfast, lunch, and dinner. Fathers, let's just tell the truth and shame the devil. If every cafeteria worker knows you by your first name, it's TIME to go. It wasn't my first name the cafeteria workers knew me by; it was my cousin who told me about his wife's birthing experience in the hospital. Let me be honest! It was me who kept going into the hospital's cafeteria eating all the pig feet, all the hogmaws, all the chitterlings. Don't pay me any mind; the hospital didn't serve those choices of food. That's one of my favorite quotes from the movie "Friday". I felt like we were at the hospital for so long it was my turn to wash the dishes. Fathers, I don't know about your hospital experience, but waiting for the doctors to discharge us took forever; I began to push the help button 15 to 20 times. I pushed the service button so much, the nurse lobby area stop replying back; I was ready to go home!

Forty-five minutes later after pushing the last service button the nurse came in and stated, "Here are your discharge papers, you're going home."

"Yay! Hip-hip hooray!" I started to sing the 1981 Stevie Wonder's "Happy Birthday" song. We began to literally throw all of our items in the baby's bag, a Ziploc bag, and any other bag I found because I didn't want the doctors to change their mind about us being discharged. While walking through the hospital halls, my wife and I stated, "We can't wait to get home so we can rest." Being first time parents, little did we know "REST" wouldn't be a part of our vocabulary for awhile.

Parenting Ain't Easy

As I was arriving to our car, strapping in the baby car seat, I felt like a CEO with a three-piece suit putting on a tire for the first time. Here I am a 6'1, 235 pound grown man and can't strap a baby's car seat in the car. So, me being the humble man I am, I decided to ask the nurse who walked us to our car for help, and she replied, "You should have asked the first time." Just joking, but the expression on her face was telling me that. Men, you know that look! It's like when you're driving with your wife or significant other you think, feel, and hope you're driving the right direction. Really, you're lost and don't want to be man enough to ask for help. So, finally when we look at our partner and ask, "Where are we?" Then they give us this look:"You should have asked the first time." Well, anyways that's another chapter called, "I can do bad all by myself, the male version."

Driving home with our beautiful daughter sitting in the car singing in the heavenly choir (and for those that don't understand, she was crying from the top of her lungs). "Ah, ah, ah, ah!!!!" I can hear the sound of Emoni's cry ringing in my ears. She was crying so loud I thought I needed to take her back to the hospital. In my opinion a baby's cry, for a mother, sounds like classical music in their ears while drinking lemonade, but for me it sound like listening to heavy metal with a migraine. This is just my opinion, that's not a statistic I researched or read; it's just how I feel. I didn't know if she was emotionally distressed, scared, or we were just bad new parents. Driving her home for the first time was like driving a brand new Hummer praying that no one would scratch, hit, bump, my new vehicle. Arriving home was a blessing, after getting all the items out the car, I felt like Dorothy off of "The Wizard of Oz," and stated, "There's no place like home!"

Holding my daughter in my hands and laying her head on my chest was an EMPOWERING moment. As I was holding her I thought about all the young men growing up, that disrespected women verbally, emotionally, and sexually, not knowing they may have a daughter one day. However, looking at the bigger picture, the young men of today don't respect women because there aren't a lot of respectable fathers at home, let alone in the community. In 1967 Aretha Franklin wrote a song called "Respect". The song refers to a strong, confident woman, who knows that she has everything her man wants. She never does him wrong, and demands his "respect". Franklin's version adds the "R-E-S-P-E-C-T." Just like in the 1967 classic, our children of today are crying out for respect from their parents.

http://thefatherlessgeneration.wordpress.com

Census Fatherhood Statistics

- 64.3 million: Estimated number of fathers across the nation

- 26.5 million: Number of fathers who are part of married-couple families with their own children under the age of 18.

Among these fathers -

  o 22 percent are raising three or more of their own children under 18 years old (among married-couple family households only).

  o 2 percent live in the home of a relative or a non-relative.

- 2.5 million: Number of single fathers, up from 400,000 in 1970. Currently, among single parents living with their children, 18 percent are men.

Among these fathers -

  o 8 percent are raising three or more of their own children under 18 years old.

  o 42 percent are divorced, 38 percent have never married, 16 percent are separated and 4 percent are widowed. (The percentages of those divorced and never married are not significantly different from one another.)

  o 16 percent live in the home of a relative or a non-relative.

  o 27 percent have an annual family income of $50,000 or more.

- 85 percent: Among the 30.2 million fathers living with children younger than 18, the percentage who lived with their biological children only.

  o 11 percent lived with step-children

  o 4 percent with adopted children

  o < 1 percent with foster children

Sacrifice

Being a parent is a blessing but takes a lot of sacrifice!!! I didn't know the weight of the sacrifice until I became a parent. I must say I have two beautiful parents who worked hard to provide for me and my siblings. My mother was a schoolteacher with Miami Dade Public Schools for 33 years, while my father worked for Sears in 1966 pumping gas for $4 an hour, then transitioned to North Miami Station Department for 30 years while being a private mechanic on the side. I can remember my father waking up at 4:30 a.m. just to iron his clothes before work. As I become older it amazed me, how my father ironed his shirt and pants to the "T" as a sanitation employee. Growing up as a child I thought food, clothes, and shelter automatically were supposed to happen! You know, lights just automatically come on, when you flip the switch; open the refrigerator and food was supposed to be present. There were many great quotes that Irene Morris stated, but one of the quotes I DIDN'T LIKE as a child, "Emerson, money doesn't grow on trees." However, when I became a man I realized money does grow on trees, it has to be processed through the government, but I know what she meant.

Parents: Time To Reflect

Question, parents!!! What is the greatest sacrifice of being a parent? Providing financial fruits for our child or providing instructions, love, and teaching them life management skills? In today's world we live in with Facebook, Instagram, Twitter, text, Linkedin, reality TV, it is such a social media fest!!! I believe social media has a big influence on the lack of time management in the homes. To all my social media lovers, I'm not against social media, especially with me being a business owner. Social media is needed and is a great marketing tool!! However, our children are crying out for that time our Facebook pagesare getting, while our children are struggling with illiteracy, identity, and low self-esteem. We as parents have to manage our offspring, which is more important than how many Twitter and Facebook followers are on our accounts. I have a good friend of mine who has six kids and four of them are adopted; he began to explain how he takes his children to the park and goes kite flying and they love to do it every week. He looked me straight in the eyes and stated, "Emerson, fathers have to understand, our children are looking for our time not our bank account."

Wow!!! I remember training a 17-year-old teenager who tore her ACL. As she began to get stronger—running 6.0 speed in her rehabilitation process for the first time in months— and excited about her progress, she wanted her mom to see her improvement in running. Parents! I don't care if your child is 2 years of age to 50 years of age: our children want our TIME instead of our MONEY! I'm not saying finances aren't important, like my father says, "No finance, no romance." And buddy! He was right. However, if it takes money to make your child behave, be happy or secure, then we as parents have another "think" coming!

Men, We're Never Too Old For Approval— During the process of writing this book, I remember reading a couple of chapters to my parents; after reading specific chapters, I was eagerly waiting to hear the thoughts from my parents. Fathers! I'm 35 years old and still thirst for approval from my parents. Fathers! When I say approval, I don't mean my parents need to tuck me in bed at night, fix my breakfast in the morning, supervise my life, hold my hand every time life becomes challenging. When I mention the word approval, I am referring to hearing them saying, "Son or daughter, job well done; if no one ever buys your book, I proud you stepped out in faith and became the first person in our linage to become an author!"Fathers the greatest approval we can ever show and say to our children is, "I love you!" Many fathers don't know how to be fathers because they never received approval from their father. I can hear a good percentage of men saying, my father was never there for me or I never met my father and I turned out all right. However, I would like to say to every man who doesn't know his father, or knows their father but doesn't have a relationship with their father, I believe we as men seek for approval from the presence of a FATHER. Example: gang association, coaches, mentors, peers, MMA, skateboarding, sports activities, or the number of women he sleeps with and his male friends saying, "you're the man!" Nevertheless, there is nothing like when we as fathers approve our child.

According to a U.S. Census Bureau report, over 25 million children live apart from their biological fathers. That is 1 out of every 3 (34.5%) children in America. Nearly 2 in 3 (65%) African American children live in father-absent homes. Nearly 4 in 10 (36%) Hispanic children, and nearly 3 in 10 (27%) white children live in father-absent homes.

The power of the blessing. Fathers when we learn that our children are seeking, searching, and screaming for our blessing, then we'll know the true meaning of being a father. Matthew 3:17:"And behold, a voice from heaven said, 'This is my beloved Son, with whom I am well pleased'."

Fathers, even Jesus Christ Himself sought approval by his father, so why do we as men think our child isn't looking for the blessing? **Blessing:1.** The act of one that blesses.**2.** A short prayer said before or after a meal; grace.**3.** Something promoting or contributing to happiness, well-being, or prosperity; a boon.**4.** Approbation; approval.

I want to speak to every man, if you are a father or not. Today, find one child you know and bless him or her with encouragement, hope, peace, favor, recognition, and love! Let me be clear in this passage: even though you may not have had your biological father in life, God will use a coach, teacher, sanitation worker, ice cream man, pastor, doctor, neighbor, mailman, uncle, brother, or step father. Understand, if you're connected with positive people, you will receive your blessing!

It's Not About Us

As fathers, we have to realize it's not about us! If we don't understand and comprehend that early, then it's going to be a Wizard-of-Oz, long, yellow, brick road journey as a parent. There are some men who'd rather keep their pride and self-centeredness more than their family. To those fathers who always win the argument with their wife, baby's mother, and children: would you rather win your argument and lose your child, wife, family, and most of all your identification in our homes? There are four seasons throughout the year. The same way seasons change throughout the course of life, parenting also has unexpected changes.

So I've been told as our kids grow, the learning seasons and lessons grow. Fathers listen! There is no PERFECT parent! Even though in the past my father made an unsound decision, my siblings and I have forgiven him because as an adult now, I realize without the right accountability any father is liable to fall. Fathers, forgive yourself and embrace your fatherhood.

After our daughter was born I learned the transition from changing the trash bag in the kitchen to my daughter's Milky Way wet, stinky pampers. What a unique adjustment it was. *I don't know who invented pampers but I know his lineage is still making royalties from his soft cotton invention.* Newborn parenting is work!!! At times the baby is crying and you don't know what she's crying about. Is she's hungry? I just fed her. Is she sleepy? She just took a nap. Is the pamper wet? I just changed it. In my opinion the newborn infancy stage is the most challenging because they can't communicate. When our daughter was within 2 to 3 months, she use to cry and I'd ask my wife what's wrong, she would state, "the baby is just sleepy." I'm like, she just woke up!!! So, I have a saying now, when someone has an attitude or angry. I say, "The baby is sleepy." Newborns are cute, adorable, but WORK! I love the 5 to 6 months stage. Matter of fact, let's go a little higher. I love one years of age, I don't know about other fathers but I can remember when Emoni was turning one. Man! That is when the child realizes they have a family. He or she recognizes you as their caregiver. Fathers, can you remember your child pulling on chairs, furniture, and anything they could get their hands on? Boy, I tell ya, those toddlers can research a home like Dora the Explorer! Pans, pots, shoes, keys, whatever they can find throughout the house, they'll find. However, we as parents understand that's the life of parenthood.

Chapter 5
DON'T LEAD BY YOUR EXAMPLES

There's an old saying, "Do as I say, and not as I do." To be honest with you, billions of men who abuse and neglect the position of father do so because they mimic their father's negative cycles. I have to say that my father is a handsome and caring man! As my siblings and I grew up, he provided for us but just like majority of men, he struggled with some issues. My father was born and raised in a small southwestern town called Cairo, Georgia. When entering into Cairo, there's a sign that says, "Welcome to Cairo, Home of Hospitality." The estimated population is 20,000. The only well known people that I knew to come out of Cairo was Jackie Robinson and Roddenberry that produced cane syrup. The local high school's mascot name is called the Syrup Makers. Cairo wasn't just a place for making cane syrup, but it was also a place where they built classic antique cars. As a child my father took us to visit his hometown. We used to pass by this produce warehouse and he stated numerous times to my siblings and I, "This is where my father took us every weekend to buy produce." As a child, when my father stated this to us, we continued to listen but became aggravated, as if we didn't remember this story last year and the year before!!! You have to understand I was born and raised in Miami, Florida. Having visited my father's hometown during my childhood, I'd gotten tired of hearing that cotton pickin' country story, but as I became older, I wanted to learn more about my father's history and childhood. They say "You never know where you're going, until you've known where you've been." My father stated, "Back then was rough times, but they didn't realize it." As I was listening to stories of my father's childhood I started to realize, my childhood stories were nothing compared to what that generation had to endure.

In the fifties education wasn't a priority in my father's household so to make ends meet, his parents made him and his brothers work instead of continuing school. My grandfather was a man I never met; he passed in 1981 and I was born in 1978. My father said he was a very patient, quiet, and hardworking man. In the 50's and 60's you had no choice but to work hard or you were spit on, beaten, or even killed. During that time they worked numerous vegetable fields for a living. Sometimes they worked one field for three to six years. After toiling the field throughout the day, they would work on another field for three to six more years, working from sun up to sun down only making $1.50—sometimes even less—an hour. The majority of the sharecrop farms had homes, and whatever field each family worked, that's the house they resided in. During that time they picked cotton, tomatoes, okra, cucumbers, and peas. Man! Today Publix has a slogan that says, "Where shopping is a pleasure." However, if my generation had to pick cotton and work from sun up to sun down for $1.50 an hour, I don't think shopping would be a pleasure! While listening to my father's childhood I slowly understood how society has changed. The men back in those times were hard workers and never looked for entitlement! The generation of men from the 70's on back was a different mindset of men! While my father's siblings picked livestock throughout the fields during the day, he began to observe his father work on cars during the weekends. As he continued to observe and listen, my father became gifted, skilled, and crafty with his hands. As he started to build on his craft he began fixing cars and building motors at the age of twelve years old, part by part, piece by piece, metal by metal, without reading a book, manual, or pamphlet. My father didn't attend a trade school, community college, or university to learn auto parts. He just observed and learned from his father, throughout time he developed in his skill. Listen! Fathers! My father didn't attend a trade school, community college, or university. He observed and learned from his father!!! I believe one of the missing links in today's generation compared to past generations is the lack of fathers representing the proper character in front of their children. I'm not saying the older generation of men was perfect but I believe when it was time to work, they worked. The generation back then didn't have room for entitlement. Men back then had to work. Some worked out of fear and others out of routine.

No Excuses

Today we have grants, internet, trade school, GED, work alliance, community college, university, and some men don't want to work. Now, to those men who have been searching and praying for employment, I'm not referring to you! I'm not writing this statement to use this platform to verbally beat a man up! I just want us to realize, if men back then can accomplish a lot with little education and information, why are the majority of us men still blaming the government, race, and economic statistics? Fathers of today! I want to speak to men in today's generation. Yes! Yes! Yes! There is injustice and sometimes it can be a demonic stronghold that's trying to stop you from breaking past that wall. However, if those men back in the 50's, 60's could survive in their time, we have no excuses other than to be an example to our generation at least with having a work ethic.

Men, I know we are living in trying times, from war in the middle east, poor economy, banks receiving bailouts, hurricanes, tornadoes, fires, floods, black-on-black crimes, identity theft, serving your full time in prison and still employers don't want to hire you because of your record, racism, prejudice, stereotypes and shootings in schools and movie theaters. In 1987 there was a song that stated, "Aight, no need to worry what the night is going to bring, it will be all over in the morning." Men, the word says in Psalm 30:5,"For his anger *endureth but* a moment; in his favour *is* life: weeping may endure for a night, but joy *cometh* in the morning." Men, let's not get our emotions on the natural elements of this world, but let's focus on endurance power. I believe there are a lot of men that have gifts within them, but never developed proper undiscovered gifts because of the absent presence of a father.

Big City

My father was raised with seventeen siblings, twelve boys and five girls. My father has many brothers, and believe me, each one of them are characters. In 1969 a couple of my father's siblings decided to move to Miami, Florida for a better living. My uncles realized the money they were making in Cairo would increase if they relocated to Miami, Florida. There is a saying, "Money makes us who we really are", and man I tell you, when my uncles left little old Cairo to Miami they acted a "straight fool." While transitioning from Cairo, GA., to Miami, Fl. was like the Lebron James taking his talents to South Beach. Please forgive me, Cleveland fans, no offense intended!

Upon arriving to Dade County, my father and his two brothers found work as Sanitation Employees for North Miami. His other three brothers fixed, built, and remodeled homes. During the day working as a sanitation employee and part time pumping gas in the afternoon at Sears. My father had an oldest brother by the name of Freeman Morris who also worked with him as a sanitation worker, but during his free time enjoyed street drag racing. Uncle Freeman was named after their father. Among my father's brothers my father stated, "Freeman, growing up, always managed and gave orders to people, he just had a way with people around him. He wasn't just a person who liked to manage, but he was a giving man." While Uncle Freeman was transporting trash back and forth with North Miami Station, he felt like this position wasn't making enough money, so he occupied his time with street drag racing and starting his auto body shop. Growing up, all of my uncles were gifted with something; if it wasn't their hands, it was their mouths. My uncles would do two things with their mouths, they would make you laugh or make you want to fight, especially if they were drunk. However, all were gifted!!!! They built homes, garages, motors, and did electrical work. They were crafty men.

Leave a Legacy

Many times I stated to my father, "If you and uncle so-and-so managed y'alls money properly, me and my cousins would've had our own Fortune 500 company!" Fathers of today, what sound financial decision are you making now to prepare your generation in the future? Ok, I'll wait for you to process that question. Yes, you're driving around with twenty-two-inch rims, gold chains, traveling all across the world, spending money in the club every weekend. However what sound decisions are you making now to prepare your generation financially and spiritually for the future? Present wealth doesn't mean anything without proper management and wisdom. Men, lets not get caught up in finances of today without having a plan for the future. Hosea 4:6:"My people are destroyed for the lack of knowledge." Without a proper plan, system, and strategy for our finances, then we lack knowledge. Also, let me say, just because you can provide a trust fund for your child doesn't mean you're leaving a spiritual inheritance!

Presently, out of twelve brothers only three are living. Men, we must teach our children how to manage money, not just make money. Romans 11:27 states "for the gift and calling of God are without repentance." I believe my father and uncles had ability to make money, but failed to teach and show their children how to maintain what they made. Fathers! Your children are going to learn more from your trade than any GED, diploma, certificate, degree and master's degree. There is an old saying, "Give a man a fish and you feed him for a day. Teach a man to fish and you feed him for a lifetime." Fathers, lets not just provide for our children, lets show them the trade and tools to provide for their own.

Proverbs 13:22:"A good man leaveth an inheritance to his children's children."

inheritance- 1.something that is or may be inherited; property passing at the owner's death to the heir or those entitled to succeed; legacy.

   2. the genetic characters transmitted from parent to offspring, taken collectively.

   3. the act or fact of inheriting by succession, as if by succession, or genetically:

   4. portion; birthright; heritage:

Fathers, let's leave an inheritance of tools, skill, wisdom, understanding, being teachable, serving, humble, patience, and character. Money comes and goes, but building character through the process of life promotes favor.

Everything Happens For a Reason

In 1965 my father settled down and got married; early in the marriage his first wife was scheduled for minor surgery, but she died during the procedure from receiving too much anesthesia. After investigating who dropped the ball during this mild procedure, my father won a lawsuit for a million dollars. And let the games begin!!! Excuse me! I shouldn't say it like that because anyone who passed before their time, it's a very sad thing! But my father, coming from a small city to a big city, receiving a million dollars is like giving my daughter a stash of money to shop in a Hello Kitty store. I wasn't living at the time, but when my father received his allocated money from the lawsuit, he bought cars, clothes, and money. In 1973 in Miami-Dade County, on a hot summer day, my father was driving a 1975 black Cadillac with white wall tires and black leather interior on 27th avenue. As he was driving he saw a slim, fair-skinned lady by the name of Irene Larkin. Blinded by the beauty on her face he stated to her, "Do you need a ride?", and her reply was, "Yes." Now let me throw out this disclaimer because I don't want people to think my mom was an escort. My mother knew of my father at church, she was a high school student when he was married to his first wife. When my mom was a teenager in high school she use to look at my father's first wife and say, "Man she shouts, screams, and falls out all the time in church, I'm glad I'm not her." Be careful of what you speak against, you maybe the next to walk in those shoes. In 1973, my parents became married, and my oldest brother was born April 1974; the beginning part of their marriage were smooth times though, it seemed on the surface. Throughout the marriage, my father traveled to numerous cities for car shows and drag racing with his brother Freeman. During that time rumors were said that my father was with other women. Meanwhile, my mom began to reject the opinions of others and continued to be committed to her husband. She just decided to block the naysayers out of her mind.

Round1

It was a normal weekend and my father was preparing to go out of town; my mother just wanted him to stay home and spend time with his family. My father felt challenged by my mother's determination of not wanting him to travel. She started to become frustrated and impatient. They began to argue from the top of their lungs, while my oldest brother began to implant seeds of silent anger, fear, and rejection. The firstborn child is special for any parent, but letting them see you fight, argue, and have other relationships outside the marriage plants negative seeds. Parents! We have to understand that our children are receiving every seed of how we interact with our mates. I don't care if he or she is the firstborn child, second child, or third. No matter how many children we have, every seed is sown, negative seeds or positive seeds. Now parents I don't want you to beat yourself up! I'm not trying to condemn you; I want to encourage you! Before you fight, punch, speak negative to your spouse, think of the seeds you're PLANTING!

When the Church Comes Together

My parents were married and attended the same church and served in respectable positions. My father was on the usher board and mother sang in the choir. While singing in the heavenly choir, my father met a lady on the usher board within the church. Men, we must always realize rejection can lead to isolation, but being married with negative accountability leads to adultery. I don't care if you're a minister, bishop, pastor, apostle, priest, deacon, or president!!!! Wrong male influence and negative accountability leads to fleshly temptation. What do I mean by fleshly? Lust! Lust of self, pride, control, stubbornness, and appetites. Fathers! When our appetites are greater than our appetite, for our mates, then adultery sits at our door.

Sunday after Sunday went by and my father began to have conversations, leading to an affair. As months went by the lady became pregnant and guess who the father is? Man, let's see if you are smarter than a 5th grader? But wait, there's more: my mother was pregnant also with me. After my mother heard of this lady's expectancy she began to congratulate her, not knowing her husband was the father. When my mother was 5 months pregnant with me (she stated to me) that's when she found out the truth, "and people wondered why I'm so outspoken." What do I mean by the word truth? My father was expecting two babies and I was born November 11, 1978 and my brother was born November 7, 1977. Wow! You talk about when the church comes together. When I was born my mom stated, "My father wasn't present at the hospital because he was in the process of leaving the home." There is an old saying, "The person you can't stand is how your child may come out looking", and let me tell you, I believe my mom probably hated my father then because I looked just like Edward Morris! Growing up my family stated I "was a black baby with pink lips." During the holidays and family reunions I got tried of hearing those same stories over and over again, "Emerson you were a BLACK tar baby, and what made it worse, your mama used olive oil as lotion for your skin, and to top that Irene dressed you and your brother with the brightest clothes." Just imagine hearing those stories during your childhood. I can hear someone say, that's traumatizing. No, please don't call Child Family Services or an attorney, that's how majority of my family members showed love and affection.

When my mother heard of the breaking news about my father's infidelity she was heartbroken. Being at a bible-believing, sound doctrine teaching church, you can expect for those Saints of the Most High God to support her and deal with truth with my father. However, during that time people at the church, family members, in-laws, co-workers, and neighbors thought she was crazy having a baby from my father, let alone being with him even though he didn't want to be with her. Now, let me clarify, not everyone thought she was insane, just majority. However, out of all the people that understood and ministered to her was a lady by the name of Sister Saunders. I called her Sister Saunders because she would be present at the church when it opened and left when it closed. I don't care if Hurricane Katrina was coming on Sunday, sister would be in church praising the Lord, while Hurricane Katrina is tearing up oak trees and flipping cars. I'm serious! Sister Saunders was such a God-fearing woman; I think Hurricane Katrina would have said, "Sister Saunders is coming to church on Sunday, so I'll hit land on Monday." She is what I call an "Old School Saint"! She'll pray a roach back from the dead. Sister Saunders had three sons: Jimmy, John, and my man Joseph. I don't know if you ever grew up with a family or friend, and you were so close with them, you thought you were related. Sister Saunders and her family supported my family in those dark times and I want to thank them!

Round 2

Many times my mom said she was done with my father, embarrassed and emotionally broken as a mother. In 1982, my baby sister Teandra Evette Morris was born. In the early part of my mother's pregnancy process, she asked God if this child can be a girl, with light skin and long hair because my brother was fair skinned and I was just pitch black. Excuse me, I meant to say dark and lovely-toned! I know it sounds weird, but some people have special prayer requests. Some women may say, "God I want to marry a man like Denzel Washington" or some men's prayer request is to "marry Halle Berry." I'm like the ESPN analyst, "Come on man!" But we all, including my mom, have special prayer requests.

However, during that time my father wasn't claiming my sister as his child stating, "That's not my child; it's someone else's child. I'm not the father." Men, it's amazing how when those girls are born our heart changes. I'm not saying we don't love our boys, but girls have father's cuddles a lot more. Maybe I say that because my firstborn is a girl. When my sister was born it seemed like my father fell in love all over again. My uncle Freeman had an auto shop and she used to shake the gate as a little girl waiting for my father to walk towards it, when my uncle saw her he would call her "Fat Gal." My father had three beautiful kids and he was a good father; however, being a husband was the last thing on his mind.

Don't Mimic What We See

Growing up from a child to a teenager, my father was a good provider; we ate Burger King, McDonalds, A &W, Kentucky Fried Chicken, man I tell you those were the days. As you can see none of those items were healthy, but they tasted delicious! At that time you didn't hear of children managing diabetes or high blood pressure, maybe because we had less video games and more outside play. During my childhood my father used to tell us, "I'm going to work on cars at the shop." As a child if your parents tell you they can fly to the moon you would probably believe them. However, as I went from kindergarten to third grade, my mom use to drive past the shop and I realized my father wasn't at the shop doing overtime. Yeah, he was putting in overtime, but not just picking up monkey wrenches overtime if you know what I mean. People always say, "What you don't know won't hurt, but the truth be told, what you do know may hurt, but will set you free." I really believe my father didn't want us to know about the things he was doing because he really did love us.

Fathers, our children aren't going to stay young forever. There will come a time in their lives when he or she wants to know the truth. I believe our children will respect us more when we communicate our mistakes we made as fathers, instead of lack of communication. As read in the beginning of this chapter, my father is a man with a lot of talents, skills, and knowledge. Just like many fathers who are reading this book have a lot of gifts, but just like all of us, including myself, sometimes we lead in bad examples! What do I mean by examples? Lack of patience, anger, fear, control, lust, lack of communication, trust, self-centeredness, etc. Fathers! Just because we saw our fathers do it doesn't mean it's right. Just because we saw our father hit our mom, use drugs, curse at us, mis-manage money, doesn't mean it's the right example. People learn by what you do, not by what you say. I believe we can change our youth today by simple talking and starting to lead. As a mentor or parent it is easy to talk but harder to lead; to be honest with you, while growing up when we got in trouble, my mom disciplined us with the belt. There was no timeout! Timeout was the leather belt. However, as a father, I'm learning the way I was beat doesn't have to be the same way I should discipline my daughter. Let me be clear! I believe in chastisement, but we as parents have to realize every example we're used to seeing doesn't have to be adopted.

Restored

While writing this chapter, "Don't Lead by Your Examples", I was very uncomfortable revealing my father's past mistakes because we all have character flaws! But I knew some males in our society today need to hear how my father made unsound decisions in his past, but later was restored! As a child, for years my mother prayed for my father to be present in the home and change from his old ways.

While months and seasons passed by, my mom decided to go back to school and study for her bachelor's degree, occupying her time with her kids, school, and church. My mother began to take her focus off of my father and focus on the bigger picture by creating a better living for her children. During that process I believe my mother still loved my father tremendously; however, focusing all of her attention on Edward Morris wasn't getting her anywhere emotionally. My mother took course by course, received credit by credit and was determined to be the first sibling in her family to graduate from college. In 1989 my mother received a four-year degree. As a child I remember that day but didn't understand the importance of it. At the graduation all my siblings and I were present while she received her bachelors, including my father. After, my mother graduated, my father started to come around. For my father making his turnaround could have been from my mother's prayers, focusing on her vision to make a better living for her kids, or just time.

Ecclesiastes 3:1:"There is a time for everything, and a season for every activity under the heavens."

Looking back, I was trying to identify what pushed my father to make a three hundred and sixty degree turn as a husband, and the only answer I came up with was time. However wives, I believe in my heart, if my mother didn't release my father to God and focus on the vision, not of herself but of her family, my father would have never took the time to see himself. Fathers! We must understand we can't be restored until we take the time to see ourselves. We as fathers, husbands, and men have to recognize restoration can't manifest in our lives if we're embracing our old hearts.

Another turning point could have been when his oldest brother Freeman Morris was murdered on July 2, 1996; my father's oldest brother, Freeman Morris, was murdered in front of his driveway. It was early Monday morning when my father woke me and my siblings to announce his oldest brother was murdered. Until this day I never saw my father mourn so silently! That murder occurred in 1996 and still to this day they haven't found the killer. In 1996 Tupac Shukar wrote a song called, "Lord Knows", and only the Lord knows if police knew the group or individuals who murdered my uncle.

Build an Early Relationship Among Your Children

During the week of preparing for my Uncle Freeman's memorial I was taking a nap over at Uncle Freeman's house and his son named Eastwood woke me up to introduce me to my father's son. I can remember Eastwood waking me up and saying, "Emerson, Emerson, wake up Emerson, your brother is here to meet you!" In my waking up I didn't need an alarm clock or mama's favorite weeping boom. I just heard my cousin say, "Your brother is here to meet you." I was anxious to see him; I woke up like Jesus called Lazarus from the dead! After, getting my vision together I didn't know to say, "Hello, what's up, I'm straight," or "you look like daddy." I was excited to meet my brother for the first time but it was strange, weird, and sad I had to meet him because of Uncle Freeman's death. Fathers, no matter what mistakes you've made, it's important to help your children build a relationship at an early age, instead of when tragedy accrues.

My brother was born November 1977 and I was born November 1978; I didn't get a chance to meet him until 1996. Wow! That's eighteen years! Eighteen years of no relationship, communication, video games, watching sports, eating together, or watching a movie. What if my father built a foundational healthy relationship early with my siblings and brother? There would be a consistent dialogue with one other. Men, we must start building healthy relationships now within your children. Strong relationships are built from the foundation of a building not the top of a roof. However fathers, we have to understand relationships can't be built on land that's not established. We must start to teach, explain, and communicate to our child who their siblings are, and no matter what unsound decisions you've made, he or she is your family. Daddy, I want to thank you for allowing me to open up this chapter so millions of men can be healed. To my siblings Tyrone, Troy, and Teandra, I love you! Men, let's adopt the positive cycles from our examples, but let's not lead by the negative cycles we have seen.

CHAPTER 6
THE GOLDEN TICKET

In the 80's there was the movie called, "Willy Wonka and the Chocolate Factory". The introduction of the movie was about thousands of children searching every candy store for a chocolate bar, hoping to see if they'd won this golden ticket so they could play within the Mr. Wonka's Castle. While thousands searched for the golden ticket, only eight kids were selected to win and experience Mr. Wonka's castle. Huh! Sounds like the NFL.

Research information from www.nflplayers.com states: "While many young people every year set their goals on becoming NFL players, it's extremely difficult to reach that level. Statistically of the 100,000 high school seniors who play football every year, only 215 will ever make an NFL roster. That is 0.2%! Even of the 9,000 players that make it to the college level only 310 are invited to the NFL scouting combine, the pool from which teams make their draft picks."

At the age of five, I played the game of football. No person or dictator was going to tell me I wouldn't have a career in the National Football League. I remember playing little league football and having to starve myself just to make weight for the game. Brother, I tell you, back then they called it discipline; however, you try that now someone will call DCF on you and the coaches! My first year I played offensive center on the ninety pound team, not knowing where to place my butt pad, and during the games I continued to jump off sides. I learned quickly that organized football was more than just a street pickup game.

In my first year we won the Super bowl and National Championship. Just adding a cherry on top of my story, I received honors for Most Improved Player on the team. For me to receive Most

Improved Player my first year was a big accomplishment! The name of our team was Scott Lake Optimists and our mascot was the Vikings. I can remember those team chats as if it was yesterday, "Give it to me one time, two times, three times, and what about that fourth time!!!" As we all padded our thigh pads ready to take the field, with the sun shining through our face masks, we thought we were NFL players. As a kid making the weight for the game was a challenge for me so I had to drink lots of water, wear a trash bag in the restroom and run the shower to its hottest temperature.

On Saturday mornings I was busy looking at college football while the University of Miami played the Florida State Seminoles in the Orange Bowl, while rushing out the door so I could make it to the game. I don't know how little league football is in other cities in America, but in "Dade County" it's like a religion! Yes! I said religion! It's like going to a funeral and you-better-wear-all-black religion! On Saturday mornings and throughout the whole day, parks were packed with the smell of fried chicken, fish, conch fitters, conch salad, conch dressings, and souse. Brother I tell you, where I'm from, those where the days. Teenagers were shooting craps, while drug dealers were making deals and searching through their beepers, making phone calls on their big block cell phones and grown men debated about who had the best little league super bowl team in their time. It wasn't just the games that were entertaining, but it was the shootouts at the park. I shouldn't say the shootouts were entertaining however; the people running from the shootouts were entertaining! I remember running for safety during a shootout at the park; I ran so fast I almost left my beautiful mother. As I began to jump the gate I heard this familiar voice say, "Emerson, you better not leave me, you know I can't jump this gate!" Her voice was beautiful but my mom was so mad these folks were shooting again, her tone sounded like that 1977 cartoon Captain Cave Man!!!!!! Believe me, then it wasn't funny but now it is! Playing five years at Scott Lake prepared me not just for football but for stick-to-it-iveness, teamwork, toughness, and leadership.

I had awesome strong coaches in my little league childhood. Each coach was totally different! Some were aggressive, loud, mellow, bold, and hands on. Looking back, a lot of them probably never played in the NFL or even attended college. However these beautiful men sacrificed their time, talents, and efforts to pour into us. I had many coaches like Coach Jackson, Coach Tard, Coach Randall, Coach Jack, Coach Tank, Coach Durant and many more. I must say out of my entire little league coaches, Coach Jackson poured into me. He wasn't just a coach but a mentor. There were many times during the summer Coach Jackson would take me and his son to cut lawns throughout Dade County. One of the areas where we cut grass was in Miami Shores. Those who live there understand Miami Shores yards weren't small! Coach Jackson would make us cut grass all day for only $25. Man, coach made a killing off of us. However, I realized he wanted to install leadership, consistency, and work ethic in us. Fathers, what are the things we're giving to our kids, and not making them work for it?

As I transitioned to high school and college, Coach Jackson's "you get what you work for" training made me a part of who I am today. Coach Jackson had a heart for young boys; it's amazing the time and energy he sowed into all us. To all the coaches around the world, please don't ignore the seeds you're sowing in your player's lives. Seeds like taking them home after a full practice with a low tank of gas, talking to them when his or her parents have given up, buying them their first tie, and most of all, sowing the seed of listening. No matter if you coach little league, middle, high school, college, and professional. Coaches, everything you do counts! To "ALL" my little league coaches who are deceased or living I want to "THANK YOU" for instilling a part of who I am today, this book can't be complete without you in my life. God bless all of you!

Your Turn to Wash the Dishes

I don't know about you but I hate washing dishes! Eating is relaxing, calm, and especially after watching a good game. However, after eating a satisfying meal, sleepy, and stomach full, then my wife says, "Ok who's going to wash the dishes?" It's like asking the mother's board, does anyone want to workout? Huh! I can hear that bold, fried-chicken-eating mother thinking,

"The devil is a liar, I believe in the spirit." As a grown man having played high school and collegiate football, it's amazing how many men support their son, nephew, cousin, brother, and mentee. However, when it comes time for PTSA, FCAT, SAT, ACT, PHONICS SOUNDS, WRITING or investing in our sons or daughters education? It's like me reacting to my wife, stating, "It's your turn to wash the dishes." Fathers, just like when someone eats a good meal in the physical, those dishes have to be cleaned or the insects and rodents will take over that kitchen and home.

As a former football player, fathers, I know it feels as if we have a restoring opportunity from our sports childhood to live through our sons, but our sons need educational fundamentals, not just fundamentals of X's and O's in a playbook. Men! I don't want to sound like a football hater; I love the game of football. Ask my wife! She knows not to bother me when USF Bulls are playing. However men, she always wants me to do something for her during that intensive drive. Wow! To death do us part. Wives, if you have a husband who loves sports, please don't interrupt him doing that important drive! Can I get at least 10 brothers who are not intimated by their wives to say a men!!! Love you, April! Fathers, mentors, uncles, bothers, friend: just like if dishes don't get washed and insects build, if we don't properly pay attention to the details of our children's education, mindset, and emotions, then we're no different than those parents in the Willy Wonka movie taking their kids to every candy store looking for the eight golden tickets.

What do I mean by the golden ticket? In the black community we have led our young males to believe that their only way to success is sports, entertainment, and drugs. Men! We have to recognize there is a widerarena than where you presently are. I didn't say where you live because you can live in a 5,000 sq. foot home, gated community, with a white gate, white horse with a gold tooth in its mouth and still be depressed or unsound. Men! I want us to understand we can live in an environment but not think or act like that environment. Let me be clear! Be proud of where you are from; embrace your culture or community. However, if you'd rather die for your block, sect or community instead of your purpose than something's wrong. Yes! There is racism, yes it feels like more injustice in our courts and law enforcement, but I hear a scripture that says "they who wait upon the Lord." Another scripture says "vengeance is mine says in the Lord." Men, in order for us to adopt the same mindset like our environments, we must educate ourselves.

Why Not You?

In Tampa, Florida, my wife and I ran a 15k and, man, it was a beast! But that's a different chapter. There were thousands of people from all ethnicities present at the race. I forgot to bring my earpiece during the run; I was thinking of songs while hearing voices at the same time, telling me to stop or our hamstrings are going to pop! I continued to run while ignoring my tiredness. During the run, I was passing many people and many people passed me. While running this 15k, I began to overhear men having conservations about stocks, equity, investments, and million dollar deals on the table. And this wasn't just one or two conversations within the run; it was numerous conversations during this run I overheard. While running I started to ponder, "If only we as African American men began teach, study, educate our sons in business, entrepreneurship, and wisdom.

Education is the first tool we need to change our mindset as fathers. When I mention the word education, I'm not just referring to book or head knowledge. I'm speaking on educating ourselves on how we were raised from our parents and what cycle I can break from what I was taught and trained. Instead of pushing our son to become athletes, lets teach them how to become an NFL owner. I can hear someone say, "That's not realistic, you know they aren't going for that." While if President Obama had listened to what they, them, or whoever said; he wouldn't be the first black President of the United States of America. Years ago they said, "man will never walk on the moon and no person will ever swim without a cage from Cuba to

Florida." Fathers, stop listening to what they say! I don't know about you, men, but if I listened to what they said, I would have never written this book. We as men have to stop waiting for people to give us direction in our God-given vision. Men, we have to stop settling for any opportunities!!! I believe the majority of male minorities never gave effort to being a lawyer, doctor, dentist, publisher, astronaut, GM of a major league team because we already had in our minds what we thought we could accomplish from the color of our skin.

Proverbs 23:7:"As a man thinketh so is he." I want to ask every man this question. What do you think of yourself? Before we can pour sound influence and instruction into our children we need to think hope, peace, and vision. Fathers! How can the blind lead the blind? You may not have a dollar to your name but if you have peace that passes all understanding, that's a healthy start for a good blood transfusion for your child. Fathers, not only what do you think of yourself, but, what do you think of your son or daughter? Do you see him or her only as a football player, basketball player, baseball player, rapper, singer, dancer, dj, etc. Fathers! There is nothing wrong with those wonderful occupations and if your son or daughter becomes a great athlete or rapper, ride it until the wheels fall off! However, let's not take their God-given gifts before they ever explore them! I never in my wildest childhood envisioned myself writing a book!!!!! I had to put five exclamation marks because I really didn't see myself as a publisher, author, writer, or translating anything of grammar let alone English!!! I struggled with reading from elementary, middle, and high school. The only interest I had was football, the weight room, and girls! Now, here we are in 2014 and I am writing a book! Wow! Men! What am I saying to you? There are gifts in you that have to be developed and the only way for that gift to be formed is through pressure. Pressure from what? There is life pressure that must test your character, finances, mindset, and more importantly, COMMITMENT! Pressure always tries an individual's full commitment. We have to let our sons and daughters go through the proper pressure in the development of life so they can tap into their gift. Before we encourage our children to shoot for the Heisman, lets teach them to shoot for the undiscovered vision within them.

The West

Growing up not only did I play football, but I loved art. From my childhood to teenage years I had wonderful teachers who instructed me on my creative skills. I was in a program called PAVAC (Performing and Visual Arts Center). The kids who were selected to be in this program were called "gifted kids." Now that I am a little wiser in my years, I realize every child is gifted or has a special gift. Once my middle school years ended, each PAVAC student had an option to apply for the high school they wanted to attend. However, just because students chose that school, it didn't guarantee he or she would be selected. One of the selected high schools that offered the PAVAC program was a school called Miami Northwestern. I was born and raised in Opa-Locka, Florida the street I grew up on was, 1336 Kasim Street 33504, so Northwestern wasn't my home school. Transitioning from middle school to high school I didn't have any familiarity with Northwestern. However, looking back at it now, we went to Liberty City numerous times for "The Martin Luther King Day Parade." When I arrived to what we know as "The West", I'VE NEVER IN MY LIFE SEEN ANYTHING LIKE IT!!! The first day of summer school my ninth grade year I thought I was in Africa! There were so many black students in one place at one time. For all my readers, if you didn't know, I'm BLACK. However, the middle school I attended had a mixture of different ethnic backgrounds, but, my first day of summer school—brother!!!! It seemed like the majority of all males wore dreads, gold teeth or even both. If you walked in the hallways you better be prepared for someone to brush against your shoulder to see what sect you claimed. In the hallway, if thugs realized you were afraid of eye contact, then other students will try you. Back in 1994 I remember my first day of summer school, once the final bell rang you saw various antique automobiles from

Chevy's, verps, dunks, drop tops, and the smell of mama's chicken truck, while students purchased Now and Laters, Twix, skittles, pig feet, slurpees, hot dogs, and soda. While the band playing The WEST's theme song with students singing in the background, "Northwestern... Highhhh we pledgeee our loyaltyyyy." Flagites, golden girls, cheerleaders and our mascot pop-locking in the middle of the field preparing for the upcoming season. Now earlier in my chapter, I stated how in Miami-Dade County football is a religion, but at The West back in the day, football was the constitution.

Nothing Is Given

No, matter what high school I was attending, I was going to play football! However, I didn't know the high school I attended had other young men that loved the game of football just like me. Trying out for junior varsity was intense and if you didn't have a strong gut, you may poop on yourself. The guys, who were trying to make the JV team, were from the Poechbeans, Allapattah, Gwen Cherry, and Brown Sub. I remember one of the boys who tried out for the team asking me, "Do you stay in the city (Liberty City)?" I stated no, "Opa-Locka." As he began to laugh, he said, "If you're not from the city, you ain't no head hunter on the field." After practicing the first three days of shirt and shorts, it was time to separate the men from the boys! Buddy, after the first day of full contact we found out quickly who was from where! After a productive full season playing on the JV team, I was selected on varsity squad and, man, let me tell you it was a WHOLE different level!!! Our coach was an old school, gray beard, clean-groomed man by the name of Coach Willie Goldsmith, a.k.a. Willie G. The man didn't play the radio, flute, piano, bass or the guitar. Anywhere on the school premises we had to have our shirts tucked in our pants. When responding or answering a question to him or the coaches it must be "yes sir, no sir." Before entering into his office we had to knock on the door and until he said, "come in", we couldn't enter in the office. Back then we thought this man was tripping. However,, me being a grown man now, I realized Coach Goldsmith had to create a different culture compared to the culture we we're accustomed to. I truly believe my transition on varsity football team made me 50% of who I am as a leader today.

What Won't Kill You, Only Makes You Stronger

When I started practicing and lifting with the varsity team I stated tomy mom, "I am sore; I can't feel my body." She said when you get to school just talk to the coach, he'll understand. So, during lunchtime there were ten veterans who played on the varsity team watching game film and I stated to Coach Goldsmith, "Today I won't be able to make it to practice." He stated, "Hell, son, why not?" My words to him were: "Because I'm sore." As those veterans in the room began to laugh from my statement to coach. I began to look at them as if they had lost their minds, because it's wasn't a laughing matter! That's when Coach Goldsmith stated, "This is a part of the process, and you are building, stretching, and forming muscles you never strengthened before." When I walked out of that office I said, "this man is crazy", but what kept me pushing is when I realized those veterans were laughing because they've been through this process before.

Men! We have to understand there are people who have been through your process of soreness before. What do I mean by process? Financial debt, loneliness, eating addictions, lust of anger, self, and trust issues. We all love the manifestation of a business, family, wealth, career, etc., but, we hate the process, time, and energy it takes to build, bulk, and breathe into business, vision, relationship, wives, and children! Manifestation is something you can touch, see, feel, hold, and walk in. However, the process has to be formed and developed! I'll repeat that again, the process has to be formed and developed! Men! When I visited my high school coach that day I didn't want to hear, "Your soreness is apart of the process, see you in practice this afternoon." I wanted to hear, "I understand your pain, come back when you feel better."

Fathers, husbands, businessmen, uncle, brother, and Waldo! When we're going through our soreness/process we have to stop looking for people to understand our pain. I really believe God places strong leaders in our life not just to build our muscles, but to build our character. Men, let's just keep it real in this chapter, majority of men loves or wish they had ripped arms, shoulders, traps, but we don't like the process of working out or changing our eating habits. Millions of men across this nation want authority, leadership, and influence, but don't want to go through the process of another man or woman in leadership telling them about the character or work ethic.

As men we must realize great leaders place a great demand. I believe I'll say that again. Great leaders place a great demand. Men, we should thank God for those tough leaders we had or have in our lives! Question? What leaders have you served/are serving and you have a disagreement with? Men, please let's not close the book now, we'll get back to the Golden Ticket. What leaders have you served or are serving, and you have a disagreement? Is it a disagreement because that leader can see past your game, hustle, slothfulness, fear of serving, fear of commitment, fear of serving under men, serving under a man who is younger than you, or serving under a man who does or doesn't have your skin tone.

> Mark 10:44-45: "And whoever wishes to be first among you shall be slave of all. For even the Son of Man did not come to be served, but to serve, and to give His life a ransom for many."Matthew 23:11: "But the greatest among you shall be your servant."

Men, if we really want to be great, learn how to serve! Serve your wife, children, community, church, family, school system, detention centers, nursing homes, serve, serve, and serve! We as men must realize we will never have people serve under us if we haven't served properly under sound leadership. Men, let's not be selfish, we can't expect people to follow our orders and we can't follow another man's orders. You can have your vision and mission statement for your business, career, and family but if you never took the time, effort, energy, and attention to serve people, you will have a long road ahead. Men, I realize the process is hard, intense, and sometimes lonely but if we learn to position ourselves under proper and sound leadership then we'll always produce the right fruit and not artificial fruit. There are many examples of artificial fruit and artificial flavors:

- Fruit Stripe-Fruit Stripe is an artificially and naturally flavored fruit chewing gum that is notorious for its strong but fleeting flavor.
- Life Savers (redirect from Fruit Juicers)-Life Savers is an American brand of ring-shaped mints and artificially fruit-flavored hard candy.
- Smarties (wafer candy)-In the United States, Smarties are a type of artificially fruit-flavored tablet candy produced by Smarties Candy Company.

As we see from our definitions. Artificial fruit tastes good but isn't always healthy for you. To have a person in leadership always making you feel good or never challenge you is like eating fruit stripes, lifesavers, and smarties. It's fun, comfortable, gives you a sugar high, but it's not healthy for your character, mindset, and vision. Healthy leadership is like ripe and whole fruit that pushes, demands, challenges, and calls forth more fruit to be developed. Growing up to this point I had some awesome, tough leaders in my thirty-five years of life. I had leaders from Edward Morris, the late Reverend W. Floyd Larkin, Coach Jackson, Coach Goldsmith, Coach Jim Levitt, and Pastor Andre V. Mitchell. Now, if you knew the names of any of these leaders I mentioned, you would understand why I'm so tough. Now my mom, Irene Morris didn't play any games either. I remember going through my teenage rebellious stages and she grabbed that kitchen knife and said, "If you keep disrespecting me in my house, I'll get your soul before God does." Needless to say, I "straightened up quickly!" I said all that to say, that was my leadership example. However, my mother's parenting wasn't always like that, just twenty percentage of the time. Men, if you have someone who is over you in leadership, who you feel is tough or pushes you out of your comfort zone, that's who you should embrace. Men, let's stop running from accountability and constructive criticism. Every leader we serve doesn't always have a problem. Out of all the jobs you've had, all your managers were racist? All your supervisors disrespected you? It comes to a point when we must take full ownership of not just our actions, but our unwilling desire to serve.

Transitioning to Varsity

During my first season on the varsity team I started my tenth grade year. Every first game of the year, the team we always played was Miami Carol City Chiefs. "The West vs. Carol City." It went down at Trash Powell Stadium. When you go to a Carol City and Northwestern game, it's like going to comedy show, club, Apollo, black beach, and seeing "Drum Line"(the movie) all at the same time. Oh, I forgot to mention, track meet because of the people running while escaping from the fights and shootouts. However, you have to be a diehard "Bull" to understand the culture. It's a "bull thang" baby, and if you're not from there, you would never understand. Now, earlier I stated you must have a strong gut when trying out for JV at The West or you will poop on yourself; however, when I started my sophomore year against Carol City, one of the biggest games on our schedule, I was so fired up, I felt like I could run straight through a wall! Back then our school didn't like Carol City and Carol City didn't like The WEST! My first year playing varsity we lost to Vero Beach in the third round playoffs. After losing to Vero Beach, our team took the bus from Vero back to Liberty City. The ride was long and silent. When we got off the bus around 2:30a.m., I remember Coach Goldsmith stating, "Be in the weight room Monday afternoon because next year we will be state champions!" Monday after school, two days after losing to Vero High, our football team trained, prepared, and worked extremely hard! Summer workouts—the heat was hotter than Tabasco sauce! We worked, and worked, until we could not work anymore. We had 21 seniors my junior year ranked number 1 in the preseason 6A polls and, buddy, you couldn't tell us anything. We were cocky! Cocky! We were so cocky the whole team wore Ken Griffey baseball cleats doing a Jamboree game, while quoting Tupac lyrics, "Shed so many tears", dancing to the song on the field. Yes! We were cocky but very talented! We had depth on offensive side and defensive side of the ball. There were some guys on our team with forty times in 4.4, 4.5; strong all across the board. Our offensive line made Sports Illustrated for having the biggest line over three hundred pounds. I can remember one college scout telling our coaches, "You guys have talent like a college team." Even though our talent was off the charts, our focus wasn't there. When we started our season we lost our first three games.

We went from talk of the town to false expectations. Many people throughout the community and newspapers were saying maybe this team was given too much hype. We started O-3, and supposed to be the best pre-season team in the state, with our backs against the wall!!!! Our community was upset, parents were upset, it was crazy! Now to all my readers, Northwestern isn't the type of high school when the football team loses, everyone says we'll get them next time. Northwestern fan supporters are die-hard, long time generational supporters. Either your great-great-grandparents attended Northwestern, or parents attended The West. During our three game losing slump, we had a group of street gangs that visited our practice; music was blasting with 25 size speakers playing out the back of their trunks, rolling six cars deep, Chevy's, verps, and trucks. As these individuals stepped out of their cars, they said with force and emotion, "Goldsmith if these boys lose one more game, that's your head." To make a long story short, we didn't lose any more games that season and won the Florida High School State Championship 1996. In Liberty City, dudes who hustle don't take their high school football team losing very well. I don't know if it's because they have a passion for football or they have five on it, like the rap group Luniz. Winning the 6A Florida State Championship was one of the greatest times in my life. It wasn't just winning state but it was being a part of a group of guys from all different backgrounds who accomplished one goal. You see, when losing to Vero Beach that night, it was disappointing. When Willie Goldsmith planted that seed of winning state for next year, we didn't believe it at first because we had never been there/saw it; however, as we continued to train, exercise, and trust one another we started to see the vision come to pass.

Plant the Seed of Life

What opportunity, scholarship, new location, calling, and revelation can your children win or possess from you planting the seed in their mind?

After we lost to Vero Beach that night, what if Coach Goldsmith got off the bus and said, "You guys can't ever win games, I wish I was at another school." Fathers, coaches, mentors, pastors, life coaches, supervisors, bosses, CEOs, children: we have the power to plant seeds of expectation in our youth, children, church, business, family, and ourselves. Men! We can't ever walk into our vision if we don't apply ourselves to focus on the task at hand. One of the tasks at hand is speaking life. We need to speak words like, "Son or daughter, you will be the next doctor, lawyer, President, principal, business owner." I believe many fathers are afraid to speak into their child's life because their father did not speak life into them. Fathers, lets put our fears to the side and speak life into our families!

Do It Right the First Time

My senior year was amazing! I was Homecoming King; captain on the football team, first-team all Dade County; life was great! However, my senior year our football team didn't do as well as my junior year. Making it to the playoffs, we lost in the first round. Disappointed by the outcome of the season I was eagerly ready for college, but I guess I failed to realize I couldn't go anywhere until I passed my SAT test. I knew I had to pass the test to get to college, but I thought I was special! To all my God-given athletes out there, please realize you aren't greater than the system. What do I mean by the system? When I mention the word system, I'm referring to Curriculum Academic Standards. The Department of Education in America has academic standards, no matter how high you can jump, run, catch, throw, hit, kick, bench, squat, you aren't greater than the academic system! Let me be clear! When a high school athlete comes up short on his or her grades, everyone always wants to point the finger at the administration or coaches. I'm not saying they shouldn't have proper accountability from their educators. However, I truly believe high school athletes should take full actions of their study habits. My senior year I didn't pass my SAT/ACT test because I didn't prepare, plan, and most of all study. In high school, the only time I focused on reading was when I wanted to look through the Miami Herald sports page. What hinders the majority of high school athletes from passing their test is lack of preparation. Athletes, if you don't plan and prepare yourself during the school semester, it's going to affect you on passing the test. Men! It's the same way in life; we can't expect to complete the test of life and we're skipping class. Skipping when proper authority tells us you're out of order and you need to study. Men, lets stop complaining, suck it up, and finish the course at hand.

During my senior year I came a couple of points short on my test; I didn't take full owner-ship of my academics. While running the streets trying to be Mr.Player, I should have looked in the mirror, put the video games down, turned off TV, and told friends, "I'm going to college so I'll talk to you at the end of the school year." It's amazing; no one ever made me workout, run sprints, or build my core when I was training for football. Only when it was time to study, I became senile. Athletes, you don't have a reading, writing, speech, or math learning disorder. You have an inconsistent studying habits disorder. Yes! I want this statement to be blunt! As athletes you need to study to show thyself approved! When I was in high school I didn't take education seriously because I didn't know the importance of it. I believe our youth of today doesn't take education serious because they don't know the importance of knowledge, job opportunities, voting, reading bills, mortgages, contracts, and most of all receiving your degree or masters.

Because of my lack of preparation for the SAT/ACT I found myself entering into University of South Florida with a prop forty-eight and taking a few courses at Hillsborough Community College. The prop forty-eight is when a University gives you three years to graduate and then after the third year, you are award another year. In the fall of 1997 was a humbling time for me, seeing a lot of my high school peers playing college football on Saturday mornings, while I had to learn the hard way by not being eligible to play for the season. Only if I would have listened from my high school freshmen to senior year within the classroom, things could have been different because my GPA would have been higher. It's very important to complete the assignments right the first time. I don't care if it's a paper test, medical checkup, whatever assignment we are given as men, we must do it right the first time! Student-athletes you have to understand, your academics aren't won when studying for the test exam, it's won during your preparation of the courses. Now, Coach Goldsmith was no joke! However, my college coach Jim Levitt was insane! Insane in a good way. When I got to USF, I said I'm going to do two years here and go straight to the league. Huh! Little did I know college was going to be a transition! Coach Levitt was intense and passionate about the game of football. Coach Levitt taught me how to be mentally tough and, man, doing my college years I needed it. I found my transition during college to be an up-and-down performer. I don't know if it was the energy it took for me to get into school that pulled the passion I had in high school or my new environment, but whatever it was, I had a decent but not great career at USF. As my senior year came up I began to train like I never did before. My bench was 425 pounds and 225 reps for 29 times. I was positioning myself because I only had a year of eligibility left. In September 2001, when playing University of North Texas in the third quarter, I broke my right tibia and fibula. I said to myself, "No, this can't be happening;" I never had a serious injury since I've played the game of football at the age of five. Why now, God? Could this have been prevented? After having a five-hour surgery and each day going by while fighting depression, not keeping food in my system, I began to lay on my back in my apartment. While the electronic machine moving front to back so my knee wouldn't stiff from the metal rod hammered through my kneecap, many of nights I thought about what's next for me. Would I get through school? Education immediately became important! As the days went by, my mother drove me to the doctor so he could take out my stitches. After leaving the doctor, I asked my mom to take me to my academic advisor to find out the status for me graduating. As my advisor began to click her mouse, scrolling through her database, she said, "Emerson, in order to graduate you need to pass 18 hours in the spring and 21 hours in the summer!" Wow! Here come the BULLS! It took me getting a prop forty-eight to get into school, now we're talking about completing all these courses, plus rehabbing my leg!!! I started to realize only if I took my education serious in high school, maybe I would not be in this predicament. At that time I finally looked myself in the mirror and said, "Emerson you have no more excuses!" Men, it took me breaking my leg and the demand of taking 18 hours in the spring and 21 hours in the summer, in order for me study, listen, focus, commit, wake up, and be a man. From countless hours of studying, praying, writing, in 2002 I graduated from University of South Florida with a criminology degree. When entering into college I never fathomed receiving my degree before leaving USF, but with the demand and accountability it was a degree in me all along. To all athletes from the inner city, rural areas and suburbs, you can accomplish any academic assignment if you ask for help, go to study hall, study groups, read, and read some more. I want to personally thank Coach Jim Levitt, Phyllis, Cindy, and Professor Browning. You guys brought the BEST out of me. Go Bulls! So fathers, before we become like the parents off the Willy Wonka and the Chocolate Factory taking our children to every candy store looking for the golden ticket, lets take our children to the library, tutoring classes, Barnes and Nobles, museums, and educational trips. After graduating from USF, I finally realized I could accomplish anything educationally, even if I wanted to write a book.

CHAPTER 7
REAL MEN DON'T CRY

Some women love to see a part of a man's sensitive side, and others can't stand to see a man crying. Especially a man that continues to cry and the family has to keep him together. However, in this chapter I will be talking about a very sensitive subject; as I was writing this book *Daddy's Milk*, God asked me a question. He stated to me, "What about the men who heard the news from the doctor, statements like, 'You guys are pregnant'!" What about the expecting father who looked at the third sonogram and the doctor stating it's going to be a boy or girl? What about the father who took time from his job painting the walls pink for his daughter or creating football shapes for his new born son? What about the father that was in the room with his wife or significant other and the same doctor who said you guys are expecting, now months later, "it's a **miscarriage**?"

To all my beautiful mothers who have experienced miscarriages, I know you're the one who conceived the child and I know you're the one whose body had to be flushed out but there are millions of men who are **silently** crying over the miscarriage just like you or even greater! As I begin to research information about men dealing with miscarriages, there weren't a lot of resources available. When I was a teenager in high school, if a young man got a girl pregnant and she had a miscarriage, nine times out of ten, he was the happiest teen in the school because he didn't want the pressure of becoming a father at an early age.

In the book of 2 Samuel Chapter 2, David and his wife Bathsheba were expecting a child, but the baby died. There was a moment in David's life where he didn't eat or drink anything because of the hurt and pain he was battling within himself. If you begin to research the text, from David's manipulating and murderous acts toward Bathsheba's first husband the child died. Millions of expecting fathers that experienced miscarriages always ask God, was it an act they committed? Was it their harsh tone towards their wife or significant other? If you're spiritual or not, to be honest with you, the majority of men that experience a miscarriage may ask God at that moment what did I do to deserve this? Or why did you allow my wife to experience this miscarriage? However, in the story it reads as David washed his face and got his self together, he encouraged himself and they had their first child by the name of Solomon who was the wealthiest man in the Bible! There are a lot of men who overcame like David, by washing their discouragement, emptiness, fear, and created their first beautiful newborn. Men, before we can encourage our wife or family, we must first learn how to encourage ourselves. Now, I'm not saying we aren't supposed to wash our face because we can't cry. As you can see in the scripture, David not only cried, he didn't eat. Men, many of us have experienced crying moments. What do I mean by crying moments? Moments like the ex-wife taking you through a divorce, losing a job, death of a parent, parents divorce unexpectedly, teenage daughter stating that she's pregnant or son stating he's addicted to drugs, blood clot, cancer, no job opportunity, and most of all losing your identity within yourself! Men, we all go through crying moments. I don't care if you arean athlete, CEO, manager, boxer, entrepreneur, and construction worker, we all go through crying moments.

By Marlo Sollitto, AgingCare.com Editor

Researchers have proven what many caregivers have already figured out on their own: sometimes there's nothing like a good cry to make you feel better.

Crying is cathartic.

Neuroscientist and tear researcher Dr. William H. Frey II, PhD, director of the Alzheimer's Disease Research Center at Regions Hospital in St. Paul, Minnesota, studies the affects of crying. He's spent over 15 years studying crying and tears.

Research shows:

- 85 percent of women and 73 percent of men felt less sad and angry after crying
- On average, women cry 47 times a year, men cry 7 times a year
- Crying bouts last 6 minutes on average
- Tears are more often shed between 7 and 10 p.m.

According to Frey, "crying is not only a human response to sorrow and frustration, it's a healthy one. Crying is a natural way to reduce emotional stress that, left unchecked, has negative physical affects on the body, including increasing the risk of cardiovascular disease and other stress-related disorders.

Here are five reasons why crying is good for you:

1.**Crying Relieves Stress**

2. **Crying Lowers Blood Pressure**

3. **Tears Remove Toxins**

4. **Crying Reduces "Manganese"**

5. **Emotional Crying Means You're Human**

Centers for Disease Control Prevention.com

Heart disease is the leading cause of death for people of most ethnicities in the United States, including African Americans, Hispanics, and Whites. For American Indians or Alaska Natives and Asians or Pacific Islanders, heart disease is second only to cancer. Below are the percentages of all deaths caused by heart disease in 2008, listed by ethnicity.[4]

Race of Ethnic Group	% of Deaths
African Americans	24.5
American Indians or Alaska Natives	18.0
Asians or Pacific Islanders	23.2
Hispanics	20.8
Whites	25.1
All	25.0

So, if Dr. Frey's data states in his research that healthy crying decreases the risk of cardiovascular disease and other stress-related disorders, men, we need to start screaming!!! Fathers, when studying this information, we need to express what's on our hearts more frequently. Question: where can a man go to get a good cry? Where can he go to show his fears, rejection, frustration, insecurities, and weakness? Oh! I know where he can go, to his high school friend, buddy or homeboy, but can't find one. What about his biological brother or sister? He can't find one. Oh, I think I found someone!

Where are his brothers in the faith? I know he'll be there for me but I can't find one. What about his drinking or smoking partner? He can't find one. The majority of men don't like sharing what's on their hearts or becoming emotional in front of their buddy's, peers, partners, friends because they maybe perceived as soft or not being a man.

Men, when I use the word cry, I'm not referring to just physically crying, but "**communicating what's on our hearts.**" Husbands!!!! I'll be the first to say, communicating with my wife is so easy when I want bedroom dessert (if you know what I mean), but communicating over the bills or our family budget is a little challenging! Conversations like, "Dear, we don't have enough to pay the bills" or "sit down, let's talk over our budget; we're in the red." Men, maybe it's just me! As an African American male the culture of communication is interesting. I know every ethnicity has its fair share of difficult dialogue but in the African

American culture, asking a man to communicate is like asking the government to lower taxes! Especially asking the man to communicate deep past insecurities or weaknesses. One thing that separates, splits, and breaks a business, church, organization, marriage, relationship, team, government, and family is lack of communication! Men, I'll be the first to own up, it's easy for many of us to communicate about sports, music, money, investments, and most of all women. However, when it comes to us being vulnerable with our wife, significant other, son, daughter, we tend to shut down or blow up. We as men don't mind communicating, just on our terms.

Men, we must ask God to help us communicate, even though our wives or significant other barks, cries, screams, or yells. As men, I believe majority of males don't communicate because our fathers or grandfathers never communicated. Now, let me be clear with my readers, every home is different!

In some homes the father did communicate but only about having sex without a condom or with a condom. Other fathers may have communicated with their daughter stating, "If you're having sex don't tell me, because I'll kill you!"

But on the other spectrum, you may have had the father who communicated, cried, and didn't know when to SHUT UP! I taught in the public schools for ten years and during that time I realized one of the most difficult things for teenage boys to do is communicate. Girls communicated and they created a gossip networking station throughout the school. Teaching in public school whenever an altercation occurred with teenage boys, I always sat down with both individuals and groups to get a better understanding. During the mediation time with those young men, ninety percent of the time it was all a misunderstanding.

http://www.pewinternet.org

The typical American teen is sending and receiving a greater number of texts than in 2009. Overall, 75% of all teens text. Here are the key findings about the role of texting in teens' lives:

- The median number of texts (i.e. the midpoint user in our sample) sent on a typical day by teens 12-17 rose from 50 in 2009 to 60 in 2011.

- Much of this increase occurred among older teens ages 14-17, who went from a median of 60 texts a day to a median of 100 two years later. Boys of all ages also increased their texting volume from a median of 30 texts daily in 2009 to 50 texts in 2011. Black teens showed an increase of a median of 60 texts per day to 80.

- Older girls remain the most enthusiastic texters, with a median of 100 texts a day in 2011, compared with 50 for boys the same age.

- 63% of all teens say they exchange text messages every day with people in their lives. This far surpasses the frequency with which they pick other forms of daily communication, including phone calling by cell phone (39% do that with others every day), face-to-face socializing outside of school (35%), social network site messaging (29%), instant messaging (22%), talking on landlines (19%) and emailing (6%).

Proper Communication

If we don't disciple our children with a proper balance of Smartphone and smart communication they will be in for a rude awaking in practical life. Let's teach our children the importance of writing letters and sitting down over lunch or dinner to discuss their day. Whatever happened to seeing the person's face you're talking to? There's nothing wrong with text or Twitter but it seems like in this day and age, the only way for individuals to receive "happy birthday", "Happy New Years", or "Merry Christmas" is through text, Twitter, or Facebook.

Question: men, do our sons or daughters follow our prideful and stubborn ways from our lack of communication?

My daughter is five years old and sometimes she cries for no reason; my reply to her is, "Emoni, what's wrong with you? Why are you crying? Learn how to communicate." Then sometimes God has to show me myself through her and says, "Emerson, you act the same way when you don't get your way." So, the question I have is: what's the difference between men who have a healthy cry compared to an unhealthy cry? The sign of an unhealthy cry is isolation, desolation, depression, suicidal, and angry crying. If you ask majority of man, "are you depressed or sad?" He may say, "man, I'm good", or if he's from around my way, he'll say, "I'm straight!" However brothers, we have to be honest with ourselves, if we don't ask for help, we'll be straight in four ways: straightjacket, court, jail, or death! I can hear someone reading that statement and saying, "You shouldn't say that, words are powerful!" I do agree life and death is in the power of the tongue. However, if we as men don't express our hearts and cry then faith without works is dead!!!! We as men would rather leave our children and family instead of communicating. We would never be able to communicate without listening. I have never, ever, seen, two people have a healthy conversation while they're talking at the same time. In order to be great communicators, we must be great listeners! If we had to leave it to our wives or significant others, they would want us to listen and not communicate at all.

Listening is the Key to Being a Healthy Crier!

Proverbs 2: [1] "My son, if thou wilt receive my words, and hide my commandments with thee;[2] So that thou incline thine ear unto wisdom, and apply thine heart to understanding;."

When counseling or mentoring, people always say, "I got it!" I may mention you need to focus on your health and they say, "I'm going to get in shape, I got it!" Get out of the unhealthy relationship, "I got it!" Go back to school, "I got it! I got it! I got it! Don't tell me anymore I got it!" We will never have it until we start doing what we said we understood. Men, I know we don't live in a perfect world, but, one of the things I do know is when I need to cry, I pray to God. Ok, I can hear someone say, "Here we go with the Easter Sunday thang!" Prayer helps me when I'm lonely, mad, upset, pissed, scared, and—can I keep it real church brothers?—even when I'm sexually aroused and my wife don't want to make love because she's sleepy and her head hurts! Lol. Husbands, don't act like I'm the only one. My wife may not like that statement, but she'll get over it after this book sells a million copies. People say why should I complain (cry)?It's not like anyone would hear me. Men, as a pastor, president of a boy's program and business owner, I cry a lot. Not from operating in multiple positions, but the sacrifice my family goes through from accepting the call. What call? The call to say yes! Yes to what? Yes to his sheep! Yes to the next generation of young males the churches or society has given up on! Yes to empower families to live healthy emotionally, physically, and nutritionally. I want every father, husband, mentor, or every male to reach for their vision. One thing that keeps me to this day (and even writing this book) is GRACE! We as men have to understand that just because we may not have a person's shoulder to cry on, God is a friend who is closer than any brother.

Matthew 27:**32:**"And as they came out, they found a man of Cyrene, Simon byname: him they compelled to bear his cross."When Jesus was sentenced to be crucified, God had a person He didn't know to help Him carry His cross. It's funny Simon didn't know he would be chosen to help Jesus carry His cross. As men, what gets us frustrated in our process of crying is: we look for the familiar people we know to help us carry our cross. Men, we have to learn how to be at PEACE when we're going through our process; God has the right Simon to help you bear the process, weight, burden, and vision. Can you imagine when Christ became tired, weak, fatigued, but his father already had a backup plan in the crowd of witness. The Simons that God has to help, support, and encourage you to carry your cross may not look like you. However, if you put your image and perspective to the side, they will understand your cry.

CHAPTER 8
WHERE IS WALDO?

⌐⌐⌐

According to the U.S. Bureau of Justice Statistics (BJS), 2,266,800 adults were incarcerated in U.S. federal and state prisons and county jails at year-end 2011—about 0.7% of adults in the U.S. resident population. Additionally,

4,814,200 adults at year-end 2011 were on probation or on parole. In total,

6,977,700 adults were under correctional supervision (probation, parole, jail, or prison) in 2011—about 2.9% of adults in the U.S. resident population.

In addition, there were 70,792 juveniles in juvenile detention in 2010.

When I was in elementary school there was this fiction book by the name *Where's Waldo?* Basically, on each page of the book you have to look attentively for Waldo or he wouldn't be found, not because Waldo wasn't within the page, but his presence wasn't clearly seen. In 2009, my parents and I visited a family member stationed at Coleman Correctional Facility in the State of Florida. As we arrived in the lobby of the prison to sign in, I was amazed by the prison's long procedures for visitors; in order to see our family we were obligated to follow these prison procedures. The correctional officer who assisted us ordered all belts, shoes, jewelry, and earrings to be taken off. The women couldn't wear short skirts or have cleavage showing. For a minute I thought we were in prison, as the officers began to gather all our belongings after we walked through the metal detector. The correctional officer stated, "Please line up on the right hand side, arm distance apart." Every visitor in that lobby was from ALL walks of life. There were different ethnicities like blacks, Latinos, and whites.

However, majority of visitors were minorities! While following the prison orders, no visitor stated, "You aren't my daddy and nobody can tell me what to do." If you wanted to see or embrace your loved one, he or she must follow those prison rules. I came to realize people follow rules and orders when it's important to them. I believe many of our youth don't follow orders because we as adults dislike orders ourselves. Parents, the way we honor authority, red lights, speed limits, and leadership, that's the way our children will honor life.

As we walked from the lobby area to the visiting area, I was amazed how many black males were incarcerated. The men in prison were from all ages. I saw young men from eighteen to grown men sixty years of age. As I began to search for my cousin, I saw someone's grandfather, uncle, brother, and father in that visiting area. In elementary school, the teacher has basic classroom rules and manners. Rules like, "raise your hand until you are called" and manners such as "thank you, yes ma'am, yes sir, no talking." In our adolescent years we think those rules and manners are simple and childish; however, those fundamental foundation rules set the standards for us as adults to respect authority. Just imagine if 80% of males in prison could have learned these fundamental rules in elementary; maybe we would have less prisons. Men, please hear my heart, I'm not saying every male in prison is there because it's their fault or can't follow rules. As we see throughout history there are men who have been falsely accused and served prison time for something they didn't do.

Warisacrime.org states:

- "An examination of the plea bargains and trials that put people behind bars ought to make clear to anyone that many of those convicted are innocent. But DNA exonerations have opened a lot of eyes to that fact. The trouble is that most convicts do not have anything that can be tested for DNA to prove their guilt or innocence. Here are 1,138 documented exonerations out of that tiny fraction of the overall prison population for which there was evidence to test. One study found that 6% of these prisoners are innocent. If you could extrapolate that to the whole population you'd be talking about 136,000 innocent people in U.S. prisons today. In the 1990s, a federal inquiry found that DNA testing, then new, was clearing 25% of primary suspects."

So, statistics show us everyone in prison isn't always guilty, but I believe those individuals who have committed the crime have a challenge in following orders. Searching for my cousin in that 1800 square foot visiting station was like trying to find my wife's money stash on a rainy day, and men you know that could be anywhere. Before I arrived to the prison, I thought the prison visitation would be intimate and secret; little did I know it was open like the Red Sea!!!!

Visitors looking for their loved ones, inmates hugging their children, wives, girlfriends, grandparents, mothers, fathers, boyfriends, man it was crazy! I vividly remember an inmate telling his son, "Make sure you do your school work, if you don't I'm going to whoop you!" The look on the little boy's face was, "If you weren't in prison I wouldn't be acting like this" or "why you didn't do your homework, like not pulling the trigger, beating on mom, selling drugs, or sexually assaulting people." Fathers, it's challenging to father our kids and not lead by example. How many of our young men and women are defiant or disrespectful to adults because they are seeking out for attention?

http://www.fathermag.com

- 85% of all youths sitting in prisons grew up in a fatherless home (Source: Fulton Co. Georgia jail populations, Texas Dept. of Corrections 1992).

Many youth act out in violence because they are crying out for attention from their fathers. In that visiting area families were eating dinner of Doritos chips and soda; for some people hearing that statement sounds sad. However, if only you were present to see the joy, content, and peace on the faces of those kids spending time with their father, uncle, cousin, brother or friend. Just like during my childhood, observing through a *Where is Waldo* book, looking attentively for Waldo on each page. I truly believe our grandmothers, mothers, wives, daughters, sisters, nieces, communities, churches, homes, and most of all our sons, asking that silent question: where is my father? In the book of Genesis

God asked Adam a question and stated, "Adam where art thou?" A father plays a very important role in the home, but especially in a child's life. I can hear that stubborn, arrogant, prideful male saying, "I live in my house! My kids, nephews, nieces, or family members see me at home every night on the couch. Look at the cell phones, clothes, and video games I purchased for them." Men, we have to understand: just because our physical bodies are present in the home, doesn't mean we're being effective fathers, uncles or mentors. Also spending money on excessive items for our children doesn't mean were pouring our knowledge, wisdom, or spirit into our offspring. Fathers we have to realize video games and clothes go out of style; however, your spiritual DNA and identification pouring into your child is priceless. Many of our youth today struggle in life because their father didn't pour his DNA and teach him or she the mistakes the he made as a person. When God asked Adam where art thou. Adam's physical body was in the garden; however, he was out of "POSITION!" If Adam stayed in position, he would have covered Eve from being deceived. Bring it into today's time, when we as men aren't there emotionally, psychologically, and spiritually for our families. Then we're out of position.

Hide and Go Seek

Growing up as a child we played this game called, "hide and go seek." The rules of the game were: you needed to choose one person as the tagger and select a **home base**. The assigned **tagger** would count the number of players and multiply that number by ten. While the selected tagger was counting, the rest of the players needed to hide somewhere at least 20 feet from base. When the tagger said, "Ready or not, here I come!" the players had to hide from the tagger and get to the base without being tagged. If all the players made it to base without being tagged, then the same person who was the tagger would be tagging again the next round. What makes hide and go seek an exciting game is it gives every player in the game a base/end point. I'll say that again, "If the player finds home base, then they're safe." Just like in the game of hide and go seek, millions of men across this nation—and especially in our prison system—are trying to hide day by day, minute by minute with social anxiety, obsessive compulsive disorder, and psychological disorders.

- Published online in APA's *Journal of Abnormal Psychology*, the study looked at the prevalence by gender of different types of common mental illnesses. The researchers also found that women with anxiety disorders are more likely to internalize emotions, which typically results in withdrawal, loneliness and depression. Men, on the other hand, are more likely to externalize emotions, which leads to aggressive, impulsive, coercive and noncompliant behavior, according to the study. The researchers demonstrated that it was differences in these liabilities to internalize and to externalize that accounted for gender differences in prevalence rates of many mental disorders.

- www.prisonreformtrust.org states. "Many prisoners have mental health problems. **72%** of male and **70%** of female sentenced prisoners suffer from two or more mental health disorders. **20%** of prisoners have four of the five major mental health disorders.**10%** of men and **30%** of women have had a previous psychiatric admission before they come into prison. Neurotic and personality disorders are particularly prevalent.**40%** of male and **63%** of female sentenced prisoners have a neurotic disorder, over three times the level in the general population. **62%** of male and **57%** of female sentenced prisoners have a personality disorder."

Men aren't only seeking for a sound base in prison, but there are millions of men who are free physically but are fighting depression, fear, suicide, anger, resentment, unforgiveness and self-abuse (rejection, low self-esteem, self-worth). I want to speak to the men who are not in prison. Just because we're free doesn't mean, we're not bound!

Ephesians 6:12:"For we wrestle not against flesh and blood, but against principalities, against powers, against the rulers of the darkness of this world, against spiritual wickedness in high places."

Men what are the issues, struggles, self-inflicting wounds you battle within yourself? Aww! Come on men, I'm not playing hide and go seek now; it's truth or dare! Can we be truthful? It's just us grown men here; what are the things that have you bound and feels like a sentence? If you have identified it, don't feel embarrassed; you're about to receive your parole! I have an older brother whose been battling with manic schizophrenia/bipolar for 12 years. When I was a junior in college, I heard of my brother's diagnoses. While researching on mental illness for this passage, I mentally went back to our childhood and tried to identify what changes accrued during my brother's adolescent years. Growing up as kids I remember my brother was antisocial majority of the time and quiet. However, as I began to mentally connect the dots from his childhood, I started to identify crucial turning points in his youth. The first turning point I believe was when he saw the mental and emotional abuse of my parent's relationship. I'm not saying my parents were always MMA fighting but maybe close to WWF. However, I believe when we as parents have negative verbal and physical communication, we emotionally and psychologically affect our kids.

www.teach-through-love.com:

- Children who see or hear their mothers being abused are victims of emotional abuse. Growing up in such an environment is terrifying and severely affects a child's psychological and social development. Male children may learn to model violent behavior while female children may learn that being abused is a normal part of relationships. This contributes to the multi-generational cycle of violence. The consequences of emotional child abuse can be serious and long-term. Emotionally abused children may experience a lifelong pattern of depression, estrangement, anxiety, low self-esteem, inappropriate or troubled relationships, or a lack of empathy.

Parents, before we expose our children to verbal and physical abuse just remember T.B.Y.S! I didn't say T.G.I.F., but T.B.Y.S. Think Before You Speak.

Think before you shake, strangle, grab, hit, degrade, talk about his or her parents, first marriage; parents just remember T.B.Y.S! It will save you time and money! Parents, we have to understand our children's spirits are open when we're having unhealthy conversations with one other. Now, I'm not saying my wife and I don't have arguments. We have to keep our heated discussions behind the scenes, not in front of our child. I believe the second turning point in my brother's childhood, when my mother approved of his second grade teacher placing him in (ESE) Exceptional Student Education for (SLD) Specific Learning Disabilities. My mother is a beautiful woman and like many of "US" as parents learn everyday from our mistakes. Like my mother always says, "When you learn better, you do better." And Lord knows, as parents we learn every moment, day, and season. Personally, I have a problem with educators labeling children in their early childhood education. I understand data is important, but before we can label them let's give each child from all economic walks of life a proper foundation on educational principles from kindergarten through third grade before we limit, cripple, and taint that child's destiny! There is a scripture in the Bible that says, "as a man thinketh in his heart so is he." If we label, position, and categorize our children at an early age in the school and home, then we're allowing their destiny to be identified as price tags at their own expense. What do I mean by price tag?

www.myfloridahouse.gov

- Services for exceptional education students are funded primarily via the Florida Education Finance Program (FEFP) through the use of basic funding, an ESE Guaranteed Allocation, and two weighted cost factors. FEFP funding reflects approximately 91 percent of the total funding for Florida's public school students. FEFP funds are calculated by multiplying the number of full-time equivalent (FTE) students in each of the funded education programs by cost factors to obtain weighted FTE students. Weighted FTE students are then multiplied by a base student allocation and by a district cost differential. In FY 2010-11, $980.5 million was appropriated to school districts through the ESE Guaranteed Allocation. Since July 1, 2000, approximately 95 percent of ESE students have generated funds at the same level as nondisabled students. These students are reported under basic programs 111 (grades PK-3 basic, with ESE services), 112 (grades 4-8 basic with ESE services) or 113 (grades 9-12 basic with ESE services). In order to fund exceptional education and related services (including therapies) for these students, an ESE Guaranteed Allocation was established by the Legislature in addition to the basic funding. The guaranteed allocation is a fixed amount provided each district.

Our children are so much greater than data, Microsoft Word, Excel, politics, systems, spreadsheets, and especially a check from state. When God said let us make man in our own image, He didn't look at statistics; He looked in the spirit, and He spoke to their potential. Our children of today are the next president, doctor, teacher, lawyer, politician, pastor, husband, wife, janitor, principal, head coach, or even astronaut. In 2003, Nas wrote a rap song and the lyrics are, "I know I can, be what I want to be, if I work hard at it, I be where I want to be."In our school system there are many beautiful people that wear different hats daily but I want all educators, teachers, guidance counselors, principals, resource officers, cafeteria workers, janitors, bus drivers, and superintendents to understand. We MUST give every student the opportunity not just to be labeled but taught, cultivated, and given an opportunity to dream. Now, let me be clear!!! **I'm not saying because your son or daughter was, or presently is, in ESE means they're not going to succeed! There are many individuals in our society who were taught in ESE classes and are doing effective things. Also, I wholeheartedly believe in ESE FUNDING FOR CHILDREN WITH SPECIAL NEEDS**.

However, I do disagree with guardians and educators who use our kids as a price tag. Parents, we should never teach our children to play crazy or insane in school just to receive a check from the state. Where I'm from we call it the crazy check. Let me reemphasize, I'm not speaking to the parents whose child has a disability. I'm speaking to those parents whose children have a sound mind, but sacrificed the child's destiny just for Mr. Benjamin. Parents, I know this is an uncomfortable topic because many people have been manipulating this negative system for so long, but just imagine what greater destiny our children will have if we allow them to walk in their potential.

Find Your Base of Peace

Throughout my brother's adolescent years he accomplished a lot. He received his driver's license, graduated with a special high school diploma, and worked as a janitor in the public schools. While working two years as a janitor, he was forced to resign for erratic behavior on the job. As time and years went by my family recognized more anger, manipulation, swearing, slamming doors, used rolls of paper towels, rolls of towel tissue, and he isolated himself in his room with the blinds closed with no light. Even now it's very uncomfortable for me personally to write about my brother's experience, because it's his testimony and I don't know how my immediate family will feel emotionally about our family's intimate story in a book. However, just like my brother, I believe there are millions of men who work nine-to-five jobs, go to school, are married, educators, counselors, millionaires, and are seeking and searching to find their base of peace, rest, understanding, joy, happiness, acceptance, and identity! Men, I don't claim to be a doctor or a therapist! Whatever your diagnosis or condition is—mental illness, physical illness, emotional illness—in order for all of us to move forward from that emotional state we must forgive. I don't care if you take prescribed medication or Flintstone vitamins, if we don't forgive people who have indirectly or directly offended, never supported, bad mouthed, or whatever. Seeker, you or I will never find our home base if we don't forgive. All men who have been diagnosed with any mental disorders: take your prescribed medication, ask God to help you through the process and with proper, wise counseling, exercise, and prayer then you will overcome your tagger and find your base of stability.

He's In School

Growing up in my community if someone we knew went to prison and you asked, "How are they doing?" The family member of that person would reply, "Oh! He's doing well; he's just up the road in school." As a child if a person said John Doe was in school, I really believed it! What they meant was he's in prison. First I must say, I don't know how it feels to be physically incarcerated. Interviewing a family member of mine who served 13 years at the age of seventeen, I understood quickly that prison wasn't the place for me. He stated he saw incidents from rape, murder, gangs, drugs, assault, you name it. While interviewing him I asked him, "How did you feel emotionally when you first arrived in prison?" He replied, "When arriving in prison I didn't want to follow the rules, especially the educational courses I needed to take." Consequently, from not following the prison rules, he was placed in a four-by-four cell many times; only one bed, toilet, sink, no phone calls, no visitations, only two meals, breakfast and dinner. During this interview as he visually took me back during this desolated era in his life; he mentioned with a serious blunt tone, "Cuz state prison is nothing to play with." At the end of the interview I asked him, what are the two scenes you remember while serving 13 years in state prison.

The two scenes he remembered were an inmate being stabbed 33 times and a nineteen year old from Atlanta, Georgia raped under his cell bed. While interviewing him I asked, "What about gangs?" His response, "Man, there's ALL types of gangs in prison and many inmates join gangs just to survive!!!"

Gangs Within the United States Prison System: An In-depth Look

Stacy J. Day, Yahoo! Contributor Network

- The formulation of gangs is becoming more and more prevalent in prisons throughout the United States. According to statistics, gang activity in prisons has increased from only 9.4 percent in 1991 to 24.7 percent in 1999 and is even higher today. I worked as a corrections officer at a maximum security women's facility in Raleigh, North Carolina as well as a medium security men's facility in Detroit, Michigan and although both men and women are part of gangs, I must say that the numbers are much higher among male prisoners. I also noticed that both prisons were very segregated, and racism is very common in prisons. Whites stuck with other whites, blacks stuck with blacks and Hispanics stuck with other Hispanics.

I have never been in a gang and I'm not familiar with gangs so I won't elaborate too much on this passage, but I'll say, men, don't try to be identified by association until you find your identity first. We as men don't know where we are until we know where we're going. When I say where you are, I'm not referring to prison location or cell number. There are many men who are not incarcerated and don't know where they are. You can be in Florida state prison, California state prison, New York state prison, and still know where you are. It's not about being physically free; it's about being free in your identity. Men, when we're free emotionally, mentally, and psychologically, that's when we're apart of the true gang which is freedom. In the children's book *Where is Waldo*, he couldn't be found until he was identified. Men, let's not be identified by your gang, hood, sect, block, but be identified by your character, obedience, and serving your time.

http://www.onlinedegrees.org/10-states-that-spend-more-on-prisons-than-education/

- **10 States That Spend More on Prisons Than Education**

  1. California: California is often cited as the worst offender when it comes to spending more on corrections than education, and it's no wonder why: the state spent $9.6 billion on prisons in 2011, but just $5.7 billion on higher education. Overall, the state spends $8,667 for each student, but about $50,000 per inmate, per year. And in the last 30 years, California has built one new college campus, but 20 new prisons. In the high-crime neighborhoods of LA, things are especially bad. More than a billion dollars are spent each year to keep residents from high-crime neighborhoods in LA, but the LA Unified School District had a deficit of $640 million in the 2010 to 2011 school year, resulting in layoffs and larger class sizes.

  2. Vermont: **Vermont** has been called out for spending more on prisons than education, to the tune of $1.37 per inmate for every $1 spent on students in the state. In 2011, the state spent roughly **$92 billion on education,** overshadowed by the

$111.3 million spent on prisons. In Vermont, each inmate costs nearly $50,000 annually. The state's prison population has doubled in size over the past decade and is expected to increase three times as fast as the general resident population over the next decade.

3. Pennsylvania: In 2009, the School District of Philadelphia fell $147 million short of its budget after losing $160 million in state funding, but at the same time, Philly taxpayers spent almost $290 million on prisons for residents from 11 of Philadelphia's neighborhoods. The balance of money for prisons vs. education is bad in Philadelphia, but it's not great in the rest of the state, either. Prisons in **Pennsylvania** edged out education by a million dollars, with **$2.1 billion going to corrections** and **$2 billion for education.** It costs more than $42,000 per year to keep a Pennsylvanian inmate in prison.

4. Delaware: For such a small state, Delaware spends quite a bit of money on its inmates: $32,967 per year, per inmate. So much so, that the expense not only matches, but exceeds what the state spends on education. In 2011, Delaware spent $212.5 in state monies for education, and $215.2 million on prisons. However, if you take away the $3.5 million spent on inmate education and training that could have been used for school kids and higher education, they're just about even.

5. Rhode Island: Another tiny state with a huge prison budget, Rhode Island spent $172.1 million on prisons in 2010. That's over $10 million more than the state contributed to education, with $161.9 billion of Rhode Island's education budget coming from the state. The small state spends more than $49,000 for each inmate every year.

6. New York: In New York State, it seems that inmates have it pretty good. The state spends a whopping average of $56,000 per year, per inmate. However, students don't enjoy the same luxuries, with $40,000 less per person as their education is

funded with just $16,000 per year from the state. New York has the honor of being the state that spends the least on education. On average, states spend 36% of their budget on education, but New York spends just 28%.

7. Michigan: keeps inmate costs lower than other states, with $28,570 spent on each prisoner per year. At the same time, students aren't getting much financial help from the state, either, with just $9,575 per year in average spending for each student. In fact, prisoners are able to take advantage of amenities like free health care, cable TV, access to a library, free sports programs, and even funding to earn a degree. Yes, you read that right: Michigan won't dish out enough money to help regular students, but they'll help foot the bill for inmates to get a college education.

8. Georgia: Amid talks of education funding cuts, Georgia's students are already suffering financially compared to the funding that inmates get. Georgia has the fourth largest prison system in the US, and inmate spending far outstrips that of student spending. The state spends $18,000 per year to house just one inmate, but only $3,800 for K-12 students. College students are allotted $6,300, but that's still just over a third of what the state has to spend for each Georgia inmate.

9. Arizona: prisons are a higher priority than education. In fact, they're a 40% higher priority. About 10 years ago, the state spent 40% more on universities than on prisons, but these days, the tables have turned: Arizona now spends 40% more on prisons than universities. How did this happen? Prison funding has gone up by 75% in the last 10 years, while university funding has declined 11%. Experts say that this spending imbalance is largely related to who's in prison, and how long they stay. All non-violent offenders in Arizona are required to serve at least 85% of their sentence. They're the only state in the country to do so, and it's a major factor in driving up prison costs.

10. Washington: spends a pretty generous amount on public school students, with a $1.5 billion budget and a per-student expenditure of about $6,500. However, compared to what the state spends on inmates, it's just a drop in the bucket. The state spends $34,500 per year, per inmate, five times as much money on prisons than schools. Experts in the state (and nationwide) are concerned that there's a "schools to prison pipeline," with an emerging trend of lower rates of graduation and higher rates of incarceration.

Maybe He Really Is In School

From researching these statistics about how many more prisons are being funded than universities, well I guess John Doe did go to school. I'm a big believer of education in prison. However, I think our government and state needs to fund more in prevention than rehabilitation. Rehabilitation is important but if we can prevent our males with solid youth programs in education, educating them on substance abuse, self-esteem classes, and emotional communication classes, then we can fund more universities, community colleges, trade schools and give our schools in every state proper resources—and just like Elementary and Secondary Education Act of 1965 (ESEA), truly we won't leave any child behind. To every man who is in prison: take advantage of every class and trade. Please use your time wisely. I don't care what sentence you received, whether it's two years, five years, ten years, twenty years or even life. Men, educate your mind with knowledge, wisdom, and truth. Study to show thyself approved. Read, read, and read again. Read about history, the justice system, prayer, love and exercise; your sentences or appeal isn't the challenge, it's the fight in your mind. People always say knowledge is power but I disagree, knowledge with applying what you've heard is power. If we don't apply we have wasted potential. Let's practice to apply! Let's practice to succeed! Men, you can win, forgive yourself and give up! To every man that's in prison I want you to know a part of *Daddy's Milk* was to give you a platform. Men, let your voices be heard—and I heard the sound of your cry, Waldo.

CHAPTER 9
MEN DON'T HAVE BREASTS

In 2009 I visited my cousin in Coleman Correction Facility and I began to explain how I'm coming out with a book called *Daddy's Milk*; he started laughing in my face, as if I was doing standup comedy for inmates. I began to ask him, "What is so funny?" He stated, "Men don't have breasts!!!!!" I was looking at him with a slight feeling of disappointment because he didn't understand the title of my book. To be honest with you, my cousin laughing at my title motivated me to complete this book and bring it to manifestation.

- In Dictionary.com the definition of breastfeed: to nurse (a baby) at the breast; suckle.
- In the medical dictionary the definition of Breastfeed: to feed (a baby) from a mother›s breast rather than from a bottle.

After arriving home at 12:15a.m. from teaching as an assistant teacher during the day with no medical insurance and Fed Ex loading packages at night, I sat in my car asking God will it get better, knowing he had a greater purpose for me and my family. As I began to find the will to get out the car from the heaviness of life, I walked up upstairs and saw my wife fighting her sleep, breastfeeding our daughter. While breastfeeding, I thought to myself, when will it be my turn? Mentally the other part of me said, that's how our daughter arrived here on God's beautiful green earth, by daddy getting his breast milk. As I reached out for my daughter wanting to hold her, she began to cry and wanted more of her mother's milk. While feeling rejected, I laid on the floor, tired emotionally and physically contemplating to myself, "What part does the father play in all of this?" Now hold on women! I can hear some women say, "Oh, you played a BIG part." Ladies I understand as fathers we put Mr. Johnson in and it's our responsibility to emotionally and mentally be apart of the breastfeeding, family, and parenting process! I'm not talking about "part" in that way. When I ask the question, "what part does the father play?" I'm asking, "as fathers when does our milk become significant or does it just spoil?"Are we truly honored as fathers or just sperm donors? Is having a child from a man important or building a family together?

When my daughter was in her infancy stage, I was a first time dad working two jobs: assistant teacher with no benefits and FedEx at night. Night after night working from sun up to sun down and then come home to find my daughter suckling on my wife breast. I stated to my wife, "There aren't a lot of books for fathers; I'm going to come out with a book." She said, "I have a title for it: *Daddy's Milk*." When she stated the title, it sounded like a kid's book. I said "*Daddy's Milk*!!! I'm not Mr. Rogers from Mr. Roger's Neighborhood; I'm Emerson from Opa-Locka, Florida." I started to ponder on the title and began studying the importance of a mother's breast milk for her child. Don't get it twisted, as my cousin alluded to, "MEN DON'T HAVE BREASTS!" However we have sperm!

Breastfeeding from the medical dictionary states: you know the benefits of breastfeeding. Breast milk contains the right balance of nutrients for your baby. Breast milk is easier to digest than is commercial formula, and the antibodies in breast milk boost your baby's immune system.

The same importance a mother's breast milk has for her child, it's just as important for a father's nourishment to his child. One of the man's "breast milks" is his name. When a baby is born the doctor cleans, weighs, and places a name band on the infant to identify him or her. If it's a single mom she may give the child her last name, but normally the baby takes on his father's last name. In the Bible when a father named his child he speaks into their destiny. In the book of Genesis God called all the animals to Adam, not for God to name them, but for Adam to name them. Men! We have the ability, life, power, and authority to name not just our children, but this fatherless generation. There is a big population of teens who have gotten involved in gangs, crimes, drugs, and sex abuse because their fathers never spoke his identity over them. Let me be clear, men! Your child inheriting your name by birth and you speaking your identity in them are two different things. Question? Emerson since you're trying to play the doctor, how can I speak my identity over my child? I'm glad you asked. The first thing our kids are looking for is love. I know we live in a technology age: Twitter, text, Facebook, or like the elderly folks call it, "Space Mountain." The times have changed and we think our youth are craving for more Wii, Xbox, and Playstation. Our children are craving, crying, and wanting more of us. Men, sometimes I'm guilty also in this area with my daughter. Staying busy trying to provide for home and managing the finances so everything can stay together like Al Green says. Men, we have to continually balance our home nourishment for our family and our careers. Men, not only does our name represent milk for our kids but our sperm does too.

In www.newsmedical.net states the term sperm is derived from the Greek word "sperma"(meaning "seed") and reproductive cells. We as fathers can't breastfeed and will never understand the breastfeeding moment between a mother and infant. However mothers, understand, realize and acknowledge!!! You would never be using that pump or breastfeeding the infant without the SPERM of that father. Yes! That's your child! Yes! You labored 12 to 15 hours in the labor room! Yes! We as men will never understand how it feels being the mother! KEEP IN MIND, IF IT WASN'T FOR THAT FATHER'S SPERM, there wouldn't be a child. Your breast wouldn't be filled with milk. I don't mean to be so passionate about this passage, but there millions of mothers that hate the smell of a man, the image of a man, and everything about a man. Why? Maybe from failed relationships with men, lack of commitment from a man, or negative experiences with their biological fathers.

Mothers, I know there are so many fathers who haven't taken responsibility as a father; however, there are some good fathers in our society who sacrifice, love, embrace and communicate with the kids every day. I didn't say perfect, but good reaching for greatness. In the process of writing this book, many women I knew thought the book was needed for men in today's society. However, from their facial expressions they didn't think many men would take the time to read it. I would question, "Why you say that?"Their reply, "You know how ya'll men are! Ya'll brothers a trip. You can't fool with ya'll sperm donors." Hearing comments like this from our beautiful sisters, I was thinking, "This is why we need a book like *Daddy's Milk*." Women, the comment I have for every woman who thinks no good of a man, "Stop having kids from a man." The man can't be that bad, sorry, and trifling if you're still having conversations with him. Ladies, I'm not trying to debate, I just want to unify our relationships, communities, homes, and most of all our children. If our mothers don't respect and honor our fathers behind the scenes, then how can our children do it publicly?

Just like breastfeeding from the medical dictionary stated breast milk contains the right balance of nutrients for your baby, breast milk is easier to digest than is commercial formula, and the antibodies in breast milk boost your baby's immune system. Men, there are millions of children who don't know the difference between our formula milk or daddy's milk. I believe formula milk is material gifts, but daddy's milk is a father's instruction. What gets "US" as fathers of today in trouble? We try to substitute material and financial items instead of teaching them proper fundamentals of patience, temperance, peace, and love. I want to speak to ALL those fathers who are hard on themselves financially or wish your family could stay in a better neighborhood. You must realize your children are being properly fed from your presence in the home instead of just giving formula, toys, clothes, and money. Now, fathers, there is nothing wrong with providing for your kids but let's not give them formula, toys, clothes, games, television, technology, shoes, cell phones, amusement parks, etc., and not give them daddy's true milk, which is you.

CHAPTER 10

Y.M.O.

⌒

In 2010 I started a boys program called Y-MO, meaning Young Men Obey. When starting this program some people thought I was insane. Not because I did the DVD workout insanity, but they stated to me, "Don't you know this generation of youth doesn't listen? If you use the name Young Men Obey these kids won't attend your program." I replied, "Why would you say that?" Their responses were, "This generation hates to obey instructions." When starting Y-MO I thought about changing the name but something in me said, "stick to what I've given you."

In the beginning process of building Y-MO was full of excitement and anxious expectations. I mentally stated, "Our young males need this type of program." Little did I know, yes, this program was needed, but finding ADULTS that have a heart for our kids was like trying to find Osama Bin Laden in a cave. I can hear some readers say, "He couldn't find anyone?" Yes, there was support from some good men. However, to help change a child's life it takes a whole community, and not just temporary volunteers! In today's generation, what's hurting our youth are temporary volunteers! Parents home today, gone tomorrow, gone today, home tomorrow; we as men need to learn commitment. To be honest with you, ladies, that's why many men don't want to get married; not because they don't love you, they're just afraid to commit. When I say it takes a whole community to raise a child, we need wisdom from the mailman, ice cream man, and every other positive male it takes to change our youth perception on a servant and respect. Now to all single mothers, please be careful of what type of males you allow to be exposed to your child. Just because he's a grown man doesn't mean that he is your son's mentor or father. Let me phrase it like this. Everything that is wrapped with bells and whistles doesn't mean it's for you! Single mothers! Your kids aren't stupid, they feel and know this current man you have in the house won't stay for long. They believe it's just a matter of time when he leaves just like Captain Sava Hook. Why do I mention Captain Sava Hook? I want to speak to our beautiful women. Don't expose your son or daughter to a man you think is early husband potential because you're building false superman ideals for that child. Beautiful ladies! I know it's tempting to have a family for your child and I know sometimes it feels empty for your kids to not have a father. Ladies, let God's timing build relationship. When a man comes into a child's life it takes trust, consistency, and time to build from temporary volunteering to daddy's milk.

When a child leaves from his or her school or afternoon program, we as parents need to do our part in the home. Well, you say, "I've tried, I'm not perfect."Parents, our kids aren't looking for perfection, they're looking for LOVE and ATTENTION. Let me be transparent, as a father myself, husband, pastor, coach business owner, and mentor. I try to balance everyday of loving my wife and daughter. I must admit sometimes it's a challenge, not because I DON'T LOVE THEM. My family is my first priority; I stated it's a challenge because I try to be superhero as a husband and father. Men! Perfection will distance you from your assignment in your child's life, but transparency will position you and your child for generations. Parents, you aren't perfect and you never will be. How many of our children will learn more from our transparency than our hypocrisy! Just like our kids say, "let's keep it real." However, parents we have to be very careful of keeping it so real that we're not changing from our unsound behavior. Example: you going to jail or prison and your child is following your footsteps. You're smoking and drinking, now your child showing you how to roll it up and take it to the head. Parents, before we can truly be transparent with our kids, we must give help from wise counseling.

During the first year of the Y-MO program, the age group was fourteen to eighteen years of age. I had two volunteer mentor coaches on staff. We studied academics, character-building skills, financial budgeting, managing, and health. Being a former physical education instructor, I believe sixty minutes of exercise is very important for our youth's emotional state of mind. When adopting a health component in our program they stated, "These kids need communication workshops to express their anger." I do agree, our youth need to be taught and shown how to express their emotions; however, if we don't give them a proper tool to release those internal toxins, there would be more communication internally within that child rather than expressing proper sound emotions through life.

About.com Exercise

Depression is so common most of us have either experienced it or know more than one person who has. Medication and therapy are common treatments, but exercise is another tool that can bring relief. Study after study has shown that exercise can fight mild to moderate depression because it:

- Increases your sense of mastery, which helps if you don't feel in control of your life
- Increases your energy
- Increases self-esteem
- Provides a distraction from your worries
- Improves your health and body, which can help lift your mood
- Helps you get rid of built-up stress and frustration
- Helps you sleep better, which can often be a problem when you're depressed

The majority of our youth today are fighting with anger, fear, hate, trust, and the absence of not just knowing their father, but having their father pour wisdom into them. I believe if we teach our youth about their internal emotions and help them socially identify those internal anger triggers into positive activities and hobbies like sports, writing, reading, music, hiking, and whatever keeps their mind occupied on their vision. I believe when our youth are occupied in safe and fun activities, few teenagers will commit violent crimes because their minds are focused on the task at hand.

During the first summer program we didn't have any funds, billboards, sponsorships, publicists, and politics. EVERYTHING WE DID THAT SUMMER WAS BY FAITH AND VISION!!! The second week of the camp we took the young men to feed the homeless. They did an excellent job; the teenagers were so amazed how many people we served were homeless. Within the program I wanted to make a clear connection by letting each male know, some of these individuals who are homeless have degrees, kids, or even had successful careers. Unexpectedly, life just took a sharp turn. Many individuals who were homeless that day approached me and stated, "Keep doing what you're doing because these young men reminds me of my son" or "if I had this program when I was a teenager I wouldn't be out here." While feeding the homeless with black beans, rice, chicken, plantains, our line went from fifteen to eighty-five people within minutes. There were so many people coming for food I thought I was at a family reunion. If you ever want to start a church and it's hard to get members, just promote food. I guess that's why Jesus had a fish fry. As the line began to dwindle more people were coming, the line went from memorial-service, single-file-straight to fighting-over-rice, earthquake-relief-in-Haiti. I really couldn't blame them; they were hungry! As we left from feeding the homeless I took the boys to an all you can eat buffet. We laughed, cracked jokes, ate plate after plate—and those boys can eat! Oh yeah, they love refills. I wanted to take them to a different environment so they can see a different side of me and the coaches. The first week of the camp was good, but when the boys became accustomed to one another it was challenging! I thought dealing with teenagers, the communication would be better because they're older. However, they were worse than elementary school kids. Short attention spans, music in their ears, slap boxing (horse play), and conversation about girls, girls, and did I say girls? Now, I was a teenager before and I played sports so I had a different mindset. Yes! I thought about girls, too, but fellas, have a balance! I guess I was the same way, but just a little mature now. There is a saying, "anything you start first will always be the tester" and brother, the first year of the program those teens tested me! Let me be clear it wasn't the boys who were frustrating, it was seeing support they weren't receiving from home. Parents before we can blame government, streets, courts system, law enforcement, white man, black man, and foreigners. We need to take full responsibility as parents!!! I know parenting isn't an easy job!!!! As a parent we deal with bills, employment, peer pressure, insurance, providing a safe living environment for our kids, making the mortgage, rent, and struggling with identity issues as a adults. We can't let the pressures of life take away our responsibilities of being a parent.

I remember one day during this summer program we went to the pool. The weather began to literally pour with severe rain; while waiting under the pool cover for the rain to stop so we could transition back to our facility, I was trying to connect with one of the boys. At home he was being defiant to his mom, but listening to his grandmother. He didn't want to stay with his mom so he continued to come in her house whenever he wanted. He was what my old high school math teacher called my classmate back in 1996: a "wannabe thug." I remember Dr. Hartfield stating those words as if it was yesterday. This young man had a mom and grand-mother supporting him, and didn't have to act like this. Even though I was reaching out to him I wasn't getting any positive signals. It was like using my Sprint phone visiting my parents in the back woods of Cairo, Georgia. I began to observe and hear the sound of the rain falling on ground. I started to become internally frustrated, saddened, angry, and tired! Apart of me was emotionally tired because I felt like I should just focus on pastoring and my own family. That little voice of doubt said, "You're wasting your time with these kids; they don't listen like people mentioned before starting this program; you don't see other pastors doing this; these boys own fathers aren't doing this; you're burning yourself out; your nonprofit program isn't even established; Y-MO isn't going to receive any grant money; its about politics; just like the rich gets richer, these established nonprofit community programs keep the funds in house." While interacting with this young man I felt a tiredness, heaviness, and hopelessness. Some people don't believe that God can speak to them but during that moment I heard the voice of God say, "When an infant poops on themselves, he or she needs their parents to change their diapers." He stated to me, "As a man, you are doing what some of their fathers should have done when they came out of the womb." Wow! I tell you revelation and clarity brings understanding. Many men quit, run, flee, and hide as a father or mentor because they don't have a revelation of their assignment in their child's life. After he spoke those words to me, I began to pour in those boys even more. Assignment, assignment, assignment! Father, what is your assignment to your child? I truly believe if every father knew their assignment as a father and walked in their proper assignment, our society wouldn't need community programs. I believe the reason why there are millions of youth programs is because many fathers in our society don't know their assignment as a father, or knows their assignment, but aren't walking in their assignment.

Assignment-

1. *something that has been assigned, such as a mission or task*

2. *a position or post to which a person is assigned*

3. *the act of assigning or state of being assigned*

Fathers the same way we're on assignment to sleep with the mother of our child, we need to be on assignment to take care of our child. There is an old saying, "you made your bed, and you need to lay in it." While I want to go a little deeper, "you have sown your seed, now its time to manage your harvest."

Year Two

After, a challenging and testing first year of Y-MO, I wasn't looking to have the second year of the program. The resources weren't there and we didn't have any funds to do what we needed. Financially, everything was coming out of my pocket; I was tired and wanted to pour into my family. Many people would ask, are you doing Y-MO program? I stated, "No." However, I began to ponder if I should do the program or not. Contemplating on continuing the program for the summer, I decided to do it, the second straight summer. During this time I met a guy on a job I was working at; he was supposed to know a wealth of knowledge about community programs. While we began to get acquainted I stated to myself, "This has to be divine connection." One month before the program, we began to meet for one hour each week about the summer. I decided to lower the age group instead of teenagers for the second year. I was expecting a good amount of students, but only five were on our list. You never know the heart of an individual until you know the character of the individual. The day before the program, I offered to pay this guy nine dollars an hour; he went off on me as if I cursed his loved one out. He stated, "This is unethical; we didn't talk about this; we're going by projected number; we're going to receive more kids. It's going to grow each week." The thing he didn't understand is this not grant funded. I'm not getting paid from this. I offered him nine dollars an hour so he didn't feel as if I was using him, but he was still stuck on getting more students—not to empower our youth, but to make his money. The first day of the camp, while I was training the boys for their one-hour fitness class, my wife was in the office showing this individual his pay that week. Little did we know he typed up a fake consultation document stating we owed him $554.00. When I saw this document I went back to 'Lil John's words, "What?

Okay!!!"Before my wife told me this information she said to herself, "God, I need your healing angel to deescalate this situation before my husband finds out about this, because my husband is going to go from 'daddy's milk' to 'daddy's-about-to-do-some-time'!" When I walked in the office to see this documentation of $554 I was just devastated and hurt, because I had to cancel the program within its second week. After experiencing that unexpected moment I said to my wife, "I'm done with trying to help people and their kids." She continued to encourage me not to stop sowing into this generation. She said, "Emerson this is your calling, this generation needs you!" I was hearing her, but wasn't hearing her; I was done! After calling each parent and giving them their money back, I began to walk to my home mailbox discouraged. I received a letter from a young seventeen-year-old male in juvenile detention center who I taught in third grade. The letter stated, "Hello Mr. Morris, I saw your article on Y-MO; I see you are still helping young males like you helped me in elementary. You know my mom that adopted me is deceased; she always spoke highly of you. I remember you and your wife fed me when I didn't have anything. Please write me back." Wow!!!!!!! I was humbled! Here I am frustrated by dishonest actions of another and God allowed a young male behind bars who I taught in third grade to pour into me.

After reading this letter I began to cry. I didn't want to continue Y-MO but receiving this letter, I knew in my heart it was not about Emerson. I want all fathers, mothers, aunts, uncles, mentors, whoever you are, to realize when we pour our time, resources, intellect, and spirit into our youth we have to UNDERSTAND IT'S NOT ABOUT US! If every adult learns how to stop being selfish and teach our assigned youth the mistakes we made, then we'll have less prisons, jails, broken homes, and gangs. Don't ever say "my son doesn't need a program", because as a parent you will never know when you may not have the answers to your child's situation. To all adults with kids or without kids don't wait for trouble to happen to your son, daughter, niece, and nephew. Let's start mentoring, pour wisdom and instructions into them now so we can develop vision instead of developing prisons.

CHAPTER 11

KING KONG AIN'T GOT NOTHIN ON ME

⌒

Before I start this chapter I MUST warn you there maybe something I say that may have you feeling uncomfortable!!! However, when writing this book I vowed in my heart to do everything in my power to bring healing in our men from all walks of life. Before writing this book my number one desire was to give EVERY man a platform for his voice to be heard, and I realize this chapter may offend religious people. I didn't say people who have relationship with God, but religious people who love surface truth but not the root of the matter. In 1933 there was this adventure film directed and produced by Merian C. Cooper and Ernest B. Schoedsack named King Kong. The film tells of a gigantic, island-dwelling, ape creature called Kong who dies in an attempt to possess a beautiful young woman. In the movie, Kong appears to be about 25 feet tall in a crouch, about seven times the height of an actual silverback gorilla. At that size, a very rough estimate tells us Kong would weigh anywhere from 20 to 60 tons.

In 2001 Denzel Washington played in a movie called "Training Day" where he played a character by the name of Alonzo. One of the scenes that really intrigued me in the movie is when the inner-city neighborhood in which he distributed drugs turned on him. One of the parts during this scene Denzel quoted, "all you m********* ha, ok alright, I'm puttin' cases on all you b****. Ha, you think you can do this ***** Jake! You think you can do this to me! You m***** **** will be playing basketball in Pelican Bay when I get finished with you!!! Shoe program n****! Twenty-three hour lock down! I'm the man up in this piece, you will never see the light, who the f*** you think you f*** with. I'm the police I run s*** here, you just live here. Yeah that's right you better walk away. Go and walk away because I'm a burn this mother f*** down. King Kong aint got s***on me!!!" Truth be told, the majority of men I know who saw Training Day stated this was their favorite part of the movie. Denzel

Washington played in numerous powerful, brilliant, and inspiring movies. However, out of all the movies he played, it's sad; he only received an Oscar for playing a gangster.

First, I want to sincerely apologize for the expletive quotes. However, I want us as men to realize we're no different than Alonzo during this scene, thinking he's greater than King Kong. Alonzo thought he was bigger than the 25-foot tall and 20 to 60-ton ape. Many of us as men from all walks of life in today's society struggle with wanting to be King Kong!!! Example: the King Kong of sleeping with multiple women; the King Kong of being the biggest drug dealer in your state, city, or block; the King Kong of murdering a person for looking at you the wrong way; the King Kong of physically, sexually, and verbally abusing women; the King Kong being the freak of nature athlete running a 4.3 in the forty yard dash and 3% body fat benching 500 pounds; the King Kong of taking steroids in MLB, NBA, NFL; the King Kong of being a pastor over a mega church and when someone asks you how many members you're seating, you say, "over 3,000";the King Kong of owning properties and investments; the King Kong in your intellectualism; and the King Kong of having multiple books published.

When I mention the word King Kong, I'm not just talking about the physical stature of a man, but I'm referring to the PRIDE of a man. Proverbs 16:18 says "pride goes without a fall." One of the things we all, as men, from bishops with preacher collars to street drug dealers, struggle with is "PRIDE". Oh, yes we do and especially we as pastors! I guess that's why God takes us all as preachers and teachers through so much stripping. Men, we must realize God will always test our pride so we can put our strength, ability, intelligence, charisma, management knowledge, and skills to Him. In high school my football team had a saying, "pain is temporary but pride is forever." When I went off to college and gave my life over to Christ, I learn within the scriptures pride will always lead to destruction. Men, can you imagine the struggle I battled with God, trying to let go of the pride and image that helped me accomplish so much? There is nothing wrong with establishing great accomplishments but men we have to give everything He favored us in to the Most High God! What made Kong so dominate was his strength; he used his strength to intimidate people. We as men have to understand pride has strength but doesn't have feeling. Pride is selfish, self-centered, and only worries about its self-worth.

Consequences in Being King Kong

Men! Yes, it seems like there are benefits in being Kong but we have to understand there are consequences in being Kong. Hey, Kong from selling drugs, in a week you made a quick 50,000 dollars in cash, but now you're serving 50 years in prison at 25 years of age and your children are missing their father's presence in the home. That is one of the consequences of being King Kong. "Kong you shot him or her pretty good," you said. "They looked at me wrong, so I'm going to kill that dude, buster, or square." Kong, you fail to realize that the consequence of murder is life in prison. Another consequence of being King Kong? You are the best player on your team and your name is always in the paper. Your nickname is "beast mode" and you have a career ending in injury; now you went from newspaper hot topic to wallpaper football shapes. Kong, you're a bad man! This is your favorite part of being Kong, a woman beater. However, Kong, you fail to recognize the consequence of hitting your baby's mother. Your daughter is observing those abusive scenes; now she allows men to do it to her. Kong, you don't care; I forgot you're Kong, you're the silverback gorilla, especially when you hit a women in the mouth. Come on Kong, really, really! Your wife or significant other has another bloody nose, split lip, and knot on her forehead. Kong, do you expect the mother's board to believe that again. What about the police, Kong? Kong makeup can cover up so much; Kong, it's time to look in the mirror.

Man in The Mirror

In 1984 Michael Jackson wrote a song called, "Man in the Mirror". One of the lyrics that stood out to me: "I'm gonna make a change for once in my life, I'm gonna feel real good, I'm gonna make a difference, I'm gonna make it right." Michael Jackson wasn't only a brilliant dancer but an awesome songwriter. When we hear this song, we nod our heads to the beat but fail to apply what we hear. How many of us as men find ourselves clapping our hands to the make a change music, but how bad do we really want to make that change? While I can hear a man saying, "how can I overcome this King Kong disease, attitude, anger, control, heart, cold, mindset, and spirit?" I believe the first way of killing the King Kong in us is by looking in the mirror and realizing, owning up, and admitting you have a problem. We as men have to realize PRIDE is when we can't see we have an issue that's holding us back from losing control. Issues of losing money, self-centeredness, and most of all losing control. Men let me stop right here for a minute. We as men have to ask God to help us with our control issues! Come on men, we can't eat our cake, ice cream, steak, and all you can eat special too! I'll first put myself on the cross then I'll come back to you. One of the controls I struggle with is the budget strategy in our house. I love giving to people and our family enjoys life, but, a part of that Kong spirit in me feels if we run out because of lack of budgeting, everybody will point the finger at the man. Now men, through God's grace, He's helping me everyday get over this Kong disease of control by coming to agreement with my wife. So, men, I just expressed a small percentage of my King Kong illness, what is your control issue? Is it controlling women emotionally or intimidation? Brothers, let's all look in the mirror, we know our disease. Come on, men, no matter what title you have please look in the mirror.

Mirror Mirror on The Wall

Kong, when you lose control, who are you, man in the mirror? If you can take your mask off just for a little bit, what would people really see? Kong, Kong, do you hear me? I asked you a question! Kong, tell me your real name. Is it Kong? Underneath these big muscles who are you? Underneath you having over 3 thousand in membership, who are you? Underneath you have a million twitter followers, who are you? Underneath your investments, who are you? Underneath all these beautiful women knocking at your door every night, who are you? Underneath your million dollar contract, who are you? Underneath these charities you give to cover up your heart, who are you? Yes, you are one of the top sponsors for that charity, but who are you? Kong! Do you hear me Kong? Kong, please don't walk away. Kong, when its time to communicate, Kong, you always walk away. Ok, thank you for staying Kong. Your family would appreciate you not leaving this time. Kong, if everything was taken from you, what will your real name be, Kong? For the sake of your daughter and son, Kong, can you make that change? What about your wife who's praying for your presence to be home, can you make that change? Kong, please turn the light back on. It's only you and I in the mirror. Its not your agent, wife, teammates, coaching staff, cabinet house, hood, gang, cell mate, covering, pastor, church, children, family or reporters. Kong, I don't want a donation from you; I just want you to turn the lights back on. Kong, I see your tears, I see you hurt just like any other man. Beyond you being 25 feet tall and 20 to 60 tons, you are human, Kong. Kong, I'm begging for you to make the change. Kong, please stop killing yourself with drugs, steroids, alcohol, gambling, and isolation from wise counseling. Kong, could you please do that? Your family is waiting. I'm waiting. I see you've stood up. No! Please don't stoop back down, oh, you need me to walk with you? Kong, I struggle with PRIDE, too, so let's walk in our new identity together.

Peek-a-boo

Wikipedia states, **"Peek-a-boo** (also spelled **peek-a-boo**) is a game played primarily with babies. In the game, the older player hides their face, pops back into the baby's view, and says Peekaboo! Sometimes followed by *I see you!* Peekaboo is thought by developmental psychologists to demonstrate an infant's inability to understand object permanence.[1] Object permanence is an important stage of cognitive development for infants. Numerous tests regarding it have been done, usually involving a toy, and a crude barrier which is placed in front of the toy, and then removed, repeatedly. In early sensorimotor stages, the infant is completely unable to comprehend object permanence."

In today's society you can't drive five minutes without seeing sexual images on billboards, ads, magazines, newspapers, bus stop, red lights, yellow lights, green lights, and all the above. There is an old joke that says, "When a woman sees a man who's attractive, she mentally takes a visual snap shot of him in her mind, but, when a man see's an attractive woman, he stares at her, from the time he sees her until she leaves his sight."

http://www.oprah.com/omagazine/Dr-Phils-MANual/2

Dr.Phil stated, "Men are visually stimulated, which means if they are in a target-rich environment, they may well become aroused. This is not just a maturity issue; their brains are actually wired that way, which is very different from your own wiring. However, this is not some involuntary reflex action over which he has no control. It is a choice. Men can be amazingly shortsighted on these issues, often failing to project ahead to the consequences of their actions on their wife or children."

In 1997 the lyrically gifted rapper Buster Rhymes had a song called, "Put your hands were your eyes can see." As men what gets us in trouble aren't our hands, feet, mouth, but our eyes!!!

www.dictionary.com

EYES-the organ of sight, in vertebrates typically one of a pair of spherical bodies contained in an orbit of the skull and in humans appearing externally as a dense, white, curved, membrane, or sclera, surrounding a circular, color portion, or iris, that is covered by a clear, curved membrane, orcornea, and in the center of which is an opening, or pupil, through which light passes to the retina.

1 John 2:16 For all that *is* in the world, the lust of the flesh, and the lust of the eyes, and the pride of life, is not of the Father, but is of the world.

Men, in this section we're going to talk about a very sensitive and vulnerable topic. It's time to put the kids to bed, and send our wives on vacation. Today's topic we're going to discuss boys, gentlemen, men, and fathers, is word called "pornography." Whoa! I'm going to tell your mama what just came out of your mouth. Come on, Emerson, do we have to talk about porn?!!!! Now you're messing with my secret stash, dog! Listen men! I'm not writing this passage to receive bonus points from the women who read this book. I can see some sisters saying, "Tell them, Emerson! My husband is porn addicted and he needs to hear this." Wait, women you stay out of our conversation and please shut the door. This is a *Daddy's Milk* class, "Adult Version." Now if you are a spiritual man and battling with pornography this maybe uncomfortable to talk about, but if you're a man whose running rampant like the Tasmanian devil, then you don't give a rats behind, you better shut your mouth. Before writing this passage a part of me said "not to go there", and another part said, "Go there, we as men need healing." I believe there are men not only in our society who are struggling with pornography, but men in our churches. From bishops with preacher collars to that brother who just gave his life over to Christ, sitting in the back pew of the church. In Mark 2:17,Jesus says, "They that are whole have no need of the physician, but they that are sick: I came not to call the righteous, but sinners to repentance."

Question: what gives a man the desire to spend thousands of dollars on porn, but then he can't pay his tithe or offering? What makes a husband or father have online teen sex chats with children and drive hundreds of miles just to sleep with them? What makes a father sleep with his own son or daughter? What makes a youth director have sexual relations with the youth, while parents entrust him or her with their kids? Men! I believe the eyes of our fleshy desires gets us in trouble. Psalms 37:4 states, "Delight thyself also in the LORD; and he shall give thee the desires of thine heart."

There are two desires: our desires and God's desires. Many of us as men have desires to be a father, husband, teacher, go to back school, or find a wife. Excuse me! I forgot it's just us as men in this classroom session today. We as men have a desire to make money, but we have to realize until we seek God through prayer WE WILL NEVER KNOW THE TRUE DESIRE OF OUR HEARTS! When we don't seek God, then we're still operating in our fairy tale, tooth fairy, lust desires. If Jesus' desire is to those who are sick, why are we as men afraid of letting Him heal us in our addictions? Men, we have to get in our spirit that He truly is God. He knows the beginning from the end, and He knows you struggle with pornography apostle, pastor, prophet, evangelist, teacher, deacon, usher, father, husband, president, CEO, manager, coach, business, and mentor. However, when we give up that one thing rich young ruler, then we will have eternal life. Sorry men! I forgot I'm not in church. I need to explain the story about the rich young ruler. Mark 10:17 says, "As Jesus started on his way, a man ran up to him and fell on his knees before him. 'Good teacher,' he asked, 'what must I do to inherit eternal life?'[18] 'Why do you call me good?' Jesus answered. 'No one is good—except God alone. [19] You know the commandments: "You shall not murder, you shall not commit adultery, you shall not steal, you shall not give false testimony, you shall not defraud, honor your father and mother."'[20] 'Teacher,' he declared, 'all these I have kept since I was a boy.'[21] Jesus looked at him and loved him. 'One thing you lack,' he said. 'Go, sell everything you have and give to the poor, and you will have treasure in heaven. Then come, follow me.'[22] At this the man's face fell. He went away sad, because he had great wealth."

Men, we all have that one thing God is calling us daily to give to Him. This is one of my favorite scriptures because the rich young ruler had a list of good things he was strong in or accomplished; however, he didn't want to see his weakness. It wasn't that Christ didn't want the rich young ruler to have money; it was never about the money! Christ knew it was a struggle for him to give up what he worshiped. Wow! That's good! The rich younger ruler could have loved drugs, alcohol, anger, fear, lack of communicating, self-centeredness, etc. Jesus would have said give that up. What is the one thing that's keeping us as men from being free from lust desires? Men, please don't walk out of class. What's the one thing keeping you from communicating, loving, or embracing your wife? Men, I don't need you to answer, I need you to think. Men, even though it's a challenge to give up that one thing, through God's GRACE and word He will help us get the process.

Trust is Broken

Ladies, I told you Daddy's Milk is having a class now. Please, ladies, stop knocking on the door. Excuse me! Mr. Black Dr. Phil wannabe! My vacation time is finished! Ask my husband this question: how did he feel when I caught him watching pornography or in his adulterous act? Daddy's Milk, after I witnessed that, all my trust for my husband was broken. The question that majority of women want to know: my husband struggles with pornography. Does he love me? Is he attracted to me? Do I sexually satisfy his needs? Now I can sense someone reading this and saying, "Is this a book for fathers or HBO late night?" Audience, please forgive me for going too deep!!!! However, it's time we as men identify these internal terminates destroying our marriages and families.

NET Nanny We Protect Families

"Porn is a purely selfish hobby—it gives nothing to anyone but the viewer and the porn producer. In that way it is not at all like other hobbies, such as painting, writing, playing a musical instrument, woodworking or gardening, which give something of value to others and make the hobbyist a more well-rounded person. With rare exception, porn for the male viewer has a singular purpose: it is a process that leads to climax. In marriage, the process leading to climax at least has the potential to be a binding, loving, giving experience for both the man and the woman. No such benefits exist with porn. In fact, when a husband is locked into the porn process leading to his private orgasms, this selfish attitude will nearly always spill over to his marriage. Over time, he will be less of a soul mate and more of an isolationist. Plus, sooner or later he will begin seeing his wife as an object similar to the porn images he views in order to achieve climax. Thus, pornography often turns intimacy in marriage into a totally selfish and narrow experience."

I believe men who struggle with masturbation or pornography don't love sex, but struggle with fear. I know many men would disagree. Now, let me be crystal clear!!!! I didn't say sex isn't good. Sex is great, and guess what? God created sex! Satan can't create sex, he can only pervert sex, but anyways, that's a demonology series. When I say fear I mean fear of commitment, communication, trust, finances, just fear.

The 5 Health Benefits of Having an Orgasm

1. Orgasms keep your girly parts healthy. The extra stimulation causes blood to rush into the genital tissue, keeping it supple and refreshed. For best results, have an orgasm at least once a week. Is it that time of the month? Studies show that having orgasms while

Aunt Flo is in town actually protects against endometriosis, a potentially dangerous uterine condition that can lead to infertility.

2. Orgasms offer powerful pain relief. Some studies suggest that a good orgasm can more than double a woman's tolerance for pain. Plus, it's an analgesic, not an anesthetic, meaning it suppresses pain without affecting sensitivity to touch — a critical ingredient when sex is on the menu.

3. Orgasms can protect your ticker. Sexual activity and orgasm are shown to reduce stress due to the surge of oxytocin, the so-called "cuddle hormone," that occurs with orgasm. What's more, studies show that orgasms lower blood pressure levels — at least among women — and high blood pressure can lead to heart attacks.

4. Orgasms help you sleep better. In addition to increasing trust, attachment and bonding, the post-O hormone oxytocin triggers a cascade of bodily events, including the release of other feel-good hormones called endorphins. These endorphins often have a sedative effect. So it's no surprise that most of us have enjoyed a fabulous night of sleep following some really great sex.

5. Orgasms can help you stay in shape and lose weight. Getting busy for 30 minutes not only heats up your honey, but it also burns calories. In fact, according to some estimates, you can torch up to 200 calories with a hot and heavy half-hour session (which theoretically — and hopefully — would include an orgasm or three).

www.self.com

Husbands, our wives should be the only orgasm that fulfills our needs. We all in life have patterns, habits, and routines. They can be positive or negative. Patterns aren't bad if they're positive tools and fundamentals to build your character; not patterns like arriving late to every function, going to bed late and waking up at 12p.m., watching television all night and sleeping all day. Negative patterns become effective over our ordained purpose and vision. We as men have to realize, even though we all have negative patterns, pornography will kill you and your family. What does a person do who struggles with overeating, drinking, smoking, drugs, depression, and pornography? Do they just pray, close their eyes and ask God for help, or do they read a scripture and wait for the scripture to come to pass? I can hear someone reading this and saying, "Wow I thought he was a pastor." Yes! I am! As a matter of fact, God called me. When I thought about this passage, "Peek-a-boo", my manuscript for *Daddy's Milk* was finished. Then God stated to me, "I want you to write about how men are struggling with images of lust in their mind." 2 Corinthians 10:5:"Casting down imaginations, and every high thing that exalts itself against the knowledge of God, and bringing into captivity every thought to the obedience of Christ."

When we, as husbands, allow our imaginations to takes over our eyes, we'll find ourselves being in multiple relationships with our wives and not knowing. Men, if we don't want to be trapped with these lust addictions then we must cover our eye gate. James 2:17:"Faith without works is dead." So, I don't want to identify the problem without having some possible solutions. Question? I have a struggle with pornography, lust, trust, or budgeting. How do I get from point A to point B with this disease? The first thing we must do to come against our lust addiction is:

1. Pray- Chronicles 7:14:"If my people, which are called by my name, shall humble themselves, and pray, and seek my face, and turn from their wicked ways; then will I hear from heaven, and will forgive their sin, and will heal their land." Now, I want

us as men not to take prayer lightly. In your time of prayer, God will reveal fresh light and revelation to the root of your issue. Men, we may think we're battling with lust but when God shows us His revelation, the root of it maybe rejection or abandonment.

2. Stay Active in Your Calling and Vision- Many times we, as men, get caught up in lust because we're not operating in our vision and we're out of position. However, you can never find vision without a continual prayer life. Our vision never stays the same that's why it's important to stay in pursuit towards God.

3. Loving Your Wife- Men, let's just be honest, we like to skip all the bases and touch home base when we're making love to our wife. However, our wives are looking for proper foreplay until every base is touched. I have been married for eight years and early in our marriage, I had to learn she loves to be touched during the day and I love to be touched at night. To be honest men, I had to learn skipping bases throughout the day keep me from touching home base at night. Come on, men, don't act like I'm the only one! You know you tried to skip some bases to get to home base. The difference between having a relationship with a person you're married to compared to a webcam show is that in a marriage you have to touch every base throughout the week; however, on a webcam, chat line, or video you can go straight to home base without a touch, smell, or taste. On the internet there's no relationship, commitment, growing old together, support; just put your hands where your eyes can see, I don't know you and you don't know me.

Husbands today I want you to look your wife in her eyes and say, "I love you." If your wife knows you struggled with pornography in the past, go to her and ask her for forgiveness. If she doesn't embrace you, don't get frustrated; show her you mean it. Men, cuts don't heal overnight and surgeries take time. Well, men that's our class for today's session. Ladies, you can now come in the class, your husbands are all yours. Remember men! Your wife can be anything you want her to be in the bedroom; you just have to touch every base during the day.

Can I Get a Spot?

Growing up as a teenager I hung out with a close friend of mine name Joseph; during the summertime, we stayed active playing numerous activities like football, basketball, wrestling, and Nintendo. When I was in seventh grade I started to lift weights with Joseph. While working out in the Miami, Florida, humid weather, our chests hung out like as if were little King Kong's. Even though we were lifting concrete weights, in my mind it felt like prison weights. When I first started weight training, I didn't know what I was doing but I wasn't going to tell JoJo because I was King Kong at thirteen years old. However, as I continued to get older and continued to train in high school, I transitioned my lifting weights from concrete to iron weights. I realized quickly doing 135 concrete weight compared to 340 iron weights were totally different! When I increased my bench weight in high school I recognized I needed a spot. What is a bench spotter? In weight training, a spotter is when an individual stands behind the bar rack supporting, encouraging, and guiding you through each intense rep. Sometimes if the weight is extremely heavy, the individual who's benching may have one person behind the bar and another individual on each side. Men listen! Depending on what weight a person is lifting, that's the number of spotters he or she needs. Men, we have to comprehend in our King Kong head, we can't ever receive a spotter in life if we're not teachable, coachable, humble, and submissive.

From playing high school to college football, I've seen a lot of guys get hurt from not having a spotter. Looking back at different incidents, it wasn't because these individuals who became injured didn't have a spot, they just didn't ask for help. King Kong, doesn't that sound like us? We have 415 pounds on the bar, and can't do 135 pounds one time. Men, the reason why it's hard for us to ask for help is because we struggle with trust issues. Well, I can hear some men say, "I don't trust man, I can do it all by myself. My daddy was never there for me! I'm a grown man." Men, we have to learn everyday how to trust or we'll be burning, stressing, and internally damaging ourselves.

Men, I'll be first to admit after my first year of pastoring my level of trusting men was out the door. I went from being open socially "wireless" to 123-lock for my password. However, in my second year, having and embracing that same mindset wasn't healthy for me. As fathers, we have to understand the greater the vision, the number of spotters you need. The greater the vision for your family the higher the accuracy of wise counseling.

You Will Need A Spot

All throughout the Bible God had spotters in place to help these many characters in the vision. Example: Moses had Jethro and Joshua, Elijah and Elisha David had Jonathan, Esther had Morcedi, Orpha had Ruth, and Jesus had the Holy Spirit. Men, I don't care if you are a bishop over an influential association or CEO over a Fortune 500 company, we all in this life are going to need a spot! Men, we have to come out of this selfish, clannish, and self-centered attitude. There was some teachers, coaches, stepfathers, mentors, pastors, cousins and friends who helped you on your fourth set in life. Oh, yes, you were approved because of your credit; you're pure because you finally have gotten over your sexual addictions, alcohol, anger, drugs, lying and financial budgeting. Men, you are successful where you're at because of the spot or spotters you've had in life.

Fathers not only do we need a spot, but our children need a spot. There are millions of grown men who are crying out everyday through drugs, alcohol, promiscuous relationships, masturbation, adultery, gambling, taking multiple college courses, because they missed the spot from their father. Men, lets get in position! None of us are perfect and Lord knows I'm not, but let's put our emotions, rejections, and selves outside of the weight room because our generation is laying on the bench hoping, observing, and praying for a spot from *Daddy's Milk*. Our sons and daughters are stating out of their mouths, "I can bench this; I can be a father as a teenager; I can be a mother as a teenager; I can take drugs it won't affect me; I'll be alright." However, if we as fathers look closely into their eyes, while they're laying on that bench of life, we'll see they're not just looking for a spot; they're looking for our presence. They want to know if this weight of life falls on me, will you still be there? Will you be there if this business, church, marriage, mortgage, addictions, ruling, or doctor's report falls on me, or will you close your eyes and act like I never needed a spot?

Now men, I'm a big believer in letting people grow and learn how to be a man because you will never understand the purpose and value of a thing if you don't know its function. We as men would never understand the value of marriage until we lose a good wife, the value of children until you can't have kids anymore. Fathers, God is trying to teach us the value of not just making babies but the value of teaching, instructing, counseling and supporting. Until we as fathers learn the importance of proper fundamentals in spotting, then in our society we'll have lower percentage of low self-esteem, social anxiety, and rejection. Men, lets open our eyes and start placing our fingertips on the bar so we can be a support, instead of always looking for someone to support us. Galatians 6:7:"Whatever a man sows he shall also reap." Whenever we spot for the people God has assigned us to, then He finds the assigned people to spot us.

CHAPTER 12
IT'S NOT TOO LATE

⌐

On June 2013, the Miami Heat were playing the San Antonio Spurs in the NBA Finals Game 6. With 7.2 seconds left, Ray Allen hit the biggest shot in Miami Heat's history. However, minutes before the franchise winning shot, Miami Heat fans left the arena with the look of disgust and disappointment. While General Manager Pat Riley was observing in the stands with the look of planning for next year's 2014 roster, the trophy was brought out from under the tunnel and yellow ropes were around the court for the championship ceremony. I'm a Heat fan, but in my eyes and fan's eyes, it was over!!! As Coach Erik Spoelstra called for the team's final time out, I was sitting home watching the game in my special orange chair; I was mentally stating to myself, "You gotta be kidding me, not 1, 2, 3, 4, 5, 6, 7 championships and these boys keep coming up short again!" However, to the fans the game was over, but to the players it wasn't over until the clock was 0.0. Men, just imagine if Lebron James would have missed the three pointer two series before Ray Allen's shot, or Chris Bosh didn't block out to grab the rebound; there would never have been a game 7.

Get In Position

Men, we have to realize it's not too late if we position ourselves in order to win! The key strategy for winning is positioning. I'll say that again! The strategy for winning is positioning. Fathers, you have 7.2 seconds left to hit the shot of reconciling with your wife, baby's mother, daughter or son. Stop looking in the past, let's look towards the future. We as men can't position ourselves when we're still saying, "I'm not going to reach out to my children because they don't call me." Come on, King Kong, we are the parent; we've sown the seed. So, it's our mandate to position ourselves in our children's education, relationship, and self-esteem. Men, we're adults now, Disney World isn't real life! If we fail to properly position ourselves, then it will be over. Yes, I said it! The game will be over. There won't be a Game 7, but, with proper positioning, boxing out, and listening, "It's never too late for us to win." Oh man, that's good!!! Fathers, I don't care if your family has written you off, it's not too late. If you have a criminal record, "It's never too late." You're receiving foreclosure notices and people called you a horrible provider, "It's never too late." You've committed adultery, "It's not too late." You've beaten your wife, "It's not too late." You were accused of being a child molester, "It's not too late." Men, do you hear me? Do you hear me?!!! Put your low self-esteem headphones down while I pass you the ball to shoot, Ray Allen. Don't give me the ball to shoot; it's your turn. There are 7.2 seconds left. "It's not too late. It's not too late. It's not too late!!!" I want to ask you a question. Who told you it's too late? Do you think it's too late? I can hear that man say, "Thanks for the pass, but I'm not qualified in this area." Come on Daddy's Milk, just bend your knees and shoot. Do you think it's too late to win your family back or gain your presence in the home? Yes, you have committed adultery. Yes, you have spent all your money on gambling, but there is 7.2 seconds left; that's just enough time for you to win your identity back. That's enough time for you to learn how to budget your finances. That's enough time to say "I'm sorry". Come on, there you go, putting on your King Kong mask again. You have 7.2 seconds; say it. Yes say, "sorry for adultery, sorry for gambling all our investments. Sorry for putting the business before the kids."

It Will Take Energy to Get Back In the Game

Men, we have to really understand even though it's not too late, the same effort and energy that got us out of position, it's going to take the same energy to get us back in the game. It's not that Ray Allen couldn't shoot; anyone who knows basketball knows he can shoot, but he made the shot when it counted. Our family knows we have the ability to love, give support, stop using drugs, stop drinking alcohol, stop sleeping with multiple women. However, they want to see can we do it went it counts. When no one is looking! What separates people who are actors in films and people who want to be actors? They produce when it counts. What separates professional athletes from other athletes? They produced when it counted in college (or whatever the organized league). Our daughters, sons, wife, or significant other are asking us to produce when it counts. Men, I can hear our children saying, "Daddy, don't just tell me you love me on my birthday, or call me when you need a ride to the liquor store and when you need money." Our children need us to produce by calling, supporting, correcting, and loving when no one else cares. As I mentioned earlier in another chapter, I never thought I would be writing a book and during this process of writing, I know without a shadow of a doubt: it's never too late to accomplish anything you want to do. There's a saying that God spoke to me in 2012, "Don't hope for it, plan for it." We as fathers, husbands, grandfathers, uncles, or just as men can conquer anything we want in our lives. However, we must have a vision and plan. Plan to win your family back, plan to become sober, plan to be healed from AIDS, cancer, diabetes, plan to get out of debt, plan to start that business, plan to be in school, plan in becoming a better reader, plan to read your word, plan to take your kids to Barnes and Nobles, plan, plan, and plan. Don't hope for it, plan for it! Men, I want to thank you for taking this journey with me from chapter 1 to chapter 12. Men, remember you are the visionary; the power is in your seed and always remember, fathers your milk does matter!

Yours truly,

Daddy's Milk

CPSIA information can be obtained at www.ICGtesting.com
Printed in the USA
LVOW09s0026160414

381852LV00008B/19/P